Contents

GROWING IN YOUR GIFTS

Carl Simmons

Group

Loveland, Colorado
group.com

Group resources actually work!

This Group resource incorporates our R.E.A.L. approach to ministry. It reinforces a growing friendship with Jesus, encourages long-term learning, and results in life transformation, because it's

Relational
Learner-to-learner interaction enhances learning and builds Christian friendships.

Experiential
What learners experience through discussion and action sticks with them up to 9 times longer than what they simply hear or read.

Applicable
The aim of Christian education is to equip learners to be both hearers and doers of God's Word.

Learner-based
Learners understand and retain more when the learning process takes into consideration how they learn best.

SEASON THREE

Growing Out: From Disciples To Disciplers

GROWING IN YOUR GIFTS

Copyright © 2010 Carl Simmons

Visit our website: **group.com**

Credits
Editor: Lee Sparks
Executive Editor: Rebecca L. Manni
Chief Creative Officer: Joani Schultz
Copy Editor: Nancy Friscia
Art Director: Paul Povolni

Cover Designer: Holly Voget
Book Designer: Jean Bruns
Illustrator: Wes Comer
Print Production: Paragon Prepress
Production Manager: Peggy Naylor

Unless otherwise indicated, all Scripture quotations are taken from the *Holy Bible,* New Living Translation, copyright © 1996, 2004. Used by permission of Tyndale House Publishers, Inc., Carol Stream, Illinois 60188. All rights reserved.

ISBN 978-0-7644-3929-2

10 9 8 7 6 5 4 3 2 1   19 18 17 16 15 14 13 12 11 10

Printed in the United States of America.

What *Growing Out* Looks Like

Growing Out is more than a series of Bible studies—it's a progression that will take you and your group from becoming disciples of Jesus to becoming disciplers of *others* in Jesus. As you move through each season, you'll grow from the inside out—and as you grow, your life in Jesus will naturally expand and branch out to others in your world.

And here's the best part: As you grow out together, you'll realize how much you're *already* discipling others—starting with those in your group!

Growing Out is designed to allow you to jump in at the most appropriate place for you and your group. To help you discover your entry point, take a look at these descriptions of each season:

Season 1: Growing in Jesus focuses on developing your relationship with Jesus. Because, let's face it, the first person you have to disciple is *yourself.* More to the point, you need to learn how to let Jesus *show* you how to be his disciple. So in this season, we focus on your relationship with Jesus and how to deepen it through spiritual disciplines such as prayer, worship, Bible study…and, not least of all, through your relationships with other Christians (such as the ones you're sitting with).

After you've been grounded in your relationship with Jesus, how does that shine into the rest of your life? That's where *Season 2: Growing in Character* comes in. This season focuses on how you can invite Jesus into your most important relationships—with your family, your friends, and the people you work with—and how to keep Jesus at the center of all of them.

Season 3: Growing in Your Gifts focuses on discovering the gifts, talents, and passions God has given you and how God might want to use them to serve others—whether that's inside or outside your church walls. After this season, you'll have a better sense of who God has created you to be and why.

And with that, you're ready for *Season 4: Growing Others.* If you've gotten this far, you've developed and deepened your walk with Jesus, you've learned how to actually live it out among those people you most care about, and you've begun to discover how God has uniquely built you. Now...how do you take what God has shown you and help *others* walk through the same process?

If you've completed Seasons 1 through 3, you already know the answer because that's *exactly* what you've been doing with your group. Season 4 will help you reach out to even more people. Call it mentoring, discipling, or just being a good Christian friend to someone who needs it, after Season 4 you'll be ready to come alongside anyone who's ready to have a deeper relationship with Jesus. Just as you were in Season 1.

In the final two seasons, you'll explore what it takes to lead others where God wants you *and* them to go next. Because as you've walked through the first four seasons, guess what? You've been growing. Others know it. And God is honoring it. So whether you see yourself that way or not, God has matured you to the point where you're ready to lead. And we're going to help you get *more* ready.

Season 5: Growing in Leadership focuses on how to stay functional even as you learn how to lead. You'll walk together through the challenges of leadership—communication, conflict resolution, building consensus, learning how to adjust your ministry, and learning to stay focused on God instead of "*your* ministry."

And as you keep growing out, God may well put things on your heart that you'll need to be the one to initiate. That brings us, at last, to *Season 6: Growing in Your Mission.* God has given you a specific vision for ministry, and now you literally need to make the dream real. We'll help walk you through the issues that come with a God-given vision. Things like, first of all, how do you know it really *is* God and not just you? How do you get others on board (and praying—a *lot*)? And how will *you* keep growing, even as the vision continues to grow and take shape?

Because, no matter where you are, you never stop *Growing Out.* God will always see to that.

Enjoy *Growing Out,* and may God bless you as you grow out together!

Why R.E.A.L. Discipleship Works

Before we go any further, go back and take one more look at the copyright page of this book (it's page 2—the one with all the credits). Go to the top of the page where it declares, "Group resources actually work!" Take a minute or two to read that entire section describing Group's R.E.A.L. guarantee, and then come back to this introduction. I'll wait for you here…

Now that we're literally back on the same page, let's explore R.E.A.L. a little more deeply. Your desire to go deeper is the reason you're reading this book, and it's not only our goal but also our *passion* to help you accomplish that desire. When it comes right down to it, there's nothing more R.E.A.L. than discipleship. Think about it:

Relational

At the heart of it, discipleship *is* relationship. First and foremost, it's about developing the most important relationship you'll ever have—your relationship with Jesus. And as your relationship with Jesus grows, it becomes far more than anything you've ever imagined.

Like any great relationship, it doesn't develop on its own. It's intentional. It's work. But it's way more than that. What we get back is far more than what we put in. How could it *not* be? It's a relationship with *Jesus.* And as that relationship grows, we'll want to bring Jesus into every other relationship we have.

So we've kept that in mind as we've designed these sessions. You'll gain a deeper understanding of God's Word, but even more impor-tant, you'll discover how to share what you've learned with those around you. And that discovery *has* to happen in community. We've made these sessions very relational because, after all, you're learning how to become disciplers. By definition, that means learning how to speak God into others' lives. As you do that, you'll get as much back as you give, if not more. Because that's what happens in great relationships.

You'll notice that we often suggest getting into pairs or smaller groups. That's because participation—and learning, not to mention life change—increases when everyone's involved. It's more challenging, sure, but it's also more rewarding. Be sure to take advantage of the times we suggest it.

All this is a long way of saying that by the time you've finished this season, not only will you have a deeper relationship with Jesus, but your spiritual relationships with others will be richer and deeper than you had ever anticipated. And when that happens, be sure to thank us; a little affirmation goes a long way toward helping us to keep doing what we do here.

Experiential

Experiences? Yeah, we've got experiences. And as you discover together where God wants to take you next, you'll have experiences of your own long after you've completed these sessions.

Research has proven again and again that the more senses we engage in the learning process, the more likely a session is to stick and truly become woven into our daily lives. Jesus knew that, too. That's why he used everyday items to make his message more real. Not only that, but he invited people out of their comfort zones to conquer their fear of the unknown. We like to do that, too. A lot.

And because it's so different from what we're used to when studying God's Word, this is often the hardest part of R.E.A.L. learning for people to embrace. Is it *really* OK to have fun when we're studying the Bible? Does it truly honor God? Wouldn't it distract us from focusing on God?

First, let's make it clear that these are legitimate concerns. I've wrestled with all of them as I've developed these sessions. We want to honor Jesus. Discipleship isn't a joke. It's serious business. It's about the rest of your life and how you'll glorify God with it. There's nothing more serious than that.

Nonetheless, sometimes the best way to get serious is to set aside our expectations first, so we're able to open up and get down to what we're *really* wrestling with, rather than just come up with the right answers, go home, and never really deal with the things God wants us to deal with. The experiences in this book go a long way toward accomplishing that. Here are just a few of the ways people "got R.E.A.L." as we field-tested this curriculum:

- A church elder in our group declared from the beginning, in no uncertain terms and with a bit of a growl, "I don't *do* games." A few weeks in, he shared, "This is exactly what [my wife and I] needed right now." Several weeks later, this same game-hating elder proclaimed, "I really *liked* that activity! It worked *perfectly!*"

- One of our hosts, who also prepared the session's snack, suggested, "I'll make sure I pull it out of the oven just when everyone gets here." She understood that not only the look and taste of the snack but also the smell would help people experience the session more acutely.

- A pastor in our group enjoyed one particular activity so much that he went ahead and used it in his own church's small-group training class.

- Another woman shared how her husband had been initially skeptical about R.E.A.L. learning and about small groups in general. (Anyone else detecting a pattern among the men, by the way?) Several sessions later, she was positively glowing as she shared how we'd "broken through" and how much he'd opened up as we'd gone along—and for that matter, how he was still talking about the session the next morning.

Discipleship *is* a lifelong adventure. And we're here to help you embrace that adventure. Together. That's why we've not only built in activities to get you thinking about your faith (and expressing it) in brand-new ways, but...well, let's just move on to...

Applicable

This is pretty straightforward. You're here not only to learn but also to grow. And that means taking what you've learned and using it.

We give you opportunities in every session to do that—to give you a safe place to experiment, if you will. We also provide opportunities at the end of each session for you to take what you've learned and "Walk It Out" in the rest of your life—so that your faith *becomes* your life, and you can take practical steps toward sharing your life in Jesus so others can see and respond to it as well.

Learner-Based

For some of you, the Bible passages and ideas you're studying may be familiar. But as you explore them in fresh ways in these sessions, you'll experience and understand God's Word in ways you've never considered before. We're studying God's living Word, after all. So we want to help you not only learn brand-new things but also find new significance and meaning in familiar and taken-for-granted ideas.

Therefore, we've been very deliberate about choosing the right approaches for the right sessions. When an activity works, let's get up and do it. If a movie clip brings out the meaning of what you're learning, throw in the DVD and let's talk. If a snack not only works as an icebreaker but also as a discussion starter about a much deeper subject, let's serve it up and dig in. And when it's time to just open up God's Word and really wrap our minds around what God wants us to understand about a given subject—or to be reminded of what God has already shown us (because we forget that all too easily, too)—then we'll bust out our Bibles and read as many passages as it takes to begin to grasp (or re-grasp) that.

You're also here to discover who *you* are in Jesus. The body of Christ is made of millions of unique parts. You're one of them. We *know* one size doesn't fit all, and we've built *Growing Out* to reflect that. So whatever reaches you best—the Bible study, the activities, the questions, the take-home pieces, whatever—use them to their fullest extent. I'll give you some more ideas of how to do this in the next two sections.

However you approach these sessions—and whether you do that as a leader or as a participant—be sure to help others in your group approach things in the ways God can best reach them. And as God works in all of you, celebrate it. A lot.

May God bless you as you begin your journey together. And as God takes each of you to the places and experiences he has prepared for you, never forget: You're all in this together. You, God, and everyone he puts in your path. And *that's* discipleship.

—*Carl Simmons*

About the Sessions

Now that you know why we do what we do, let's talk about *how* we do it—and more important—how *you* can do it.

You may already understand this, but just so we're clear: Discipleship is *not* about completing a curriculum. It's about developing and deepening the most important spiritual relationships you have—first with God, then with those God brings you in contact with—because *none* of those relationships is an accident. They're all intentional, and we need to be intentional as well.

In fact, that's why we refer to each study as a season, rather than as a study, book, or quarter. We each grow at our own pace. Your season of growth might be longer or shorter than someone else's, and that's OK. God will take as long as you need to get you where he wants you. So spend as much time in each season as you need to. But stay committed to moving forward.

Also, each season has been built so that whether you're a participant or a leader, you can get the most out of each session. And that starts with the layout of each lesson. Keep a finger here, flip over to one of the sessions, and let's look at why this is so different.

This isn't just a leader guide. It's not just a guide for group members. It's *both!* And the way we've set up the sessions reflects that.

Leaders: The left-hand pages contain *your* instructions, so you're constantly on track and know what's happening next. What you do, what you say—all the basics are there. You'll also want to be sure to check out the "Leader Notes" beginning on page 185—they'll give you specific prep instructions for each session as well as great tips to make each session the best it can be.

Group Members: You don't care about all that leader stuff, do you? Didn't think so. Now you don't need to. The right-hand pages are just for you. Write your answers, journal whatever else God is saying to you, record insights from your group discussions, doodle while you listen—you've got plenty of room for all of it. All the questions and Bible passages you'll be using are right there. Use your pages to get the most out of what God is showing you each week.

Got all that? Good. Now let's talk about what each session looks like.

Come and See

In this (usually) brief opening section, you'll take time to unwind and transition from wherever you're coming from—a hectic drive to church on a Sunday morning or the end of a busy day—into the theme of the session. You and your group might enjoy a snack or a movie clip together; maybe it'll be an activity; maybe you'll just talk with someone else. Then you'll be ready to dig in deep. And maybe—because you were too busy having such a good time doing it—you won't even realize that you've already gotten down to business.

Seek and Find

This is the heart of each session and usually the longest section. You'll spend roughly a half-hour digging into God's Word and discovering its meaning in a way you hadn't realized before. You think you understand these things now? Just *wait*. Through a variety of experiences and powerful questions that take a fresh look both at Scripture and at what's going on in your own head and heart, you'll discover how God's Word *really* applies to your life.

Go

Now you'll move from understanding how what you've been studying applies to your life to considering ways to act on it. Again, through meaningful experiences and questions, you'll discover what you can do with what God has shown you through today's session. Which will take you directly into...

Walk It Out

This is the take-home part of the session. With a partner or partners, you'll each choose a weekly challenge to apply this session to your life in practical ways in the coming week and beyond.

We've broken out the challenges very specifically, to meet you wherever you are:

☐ **know it** Some of you are visual learners—you get it by reading it. Others of you just don't feel comfortable being "outward" in your faith yet. This section's for you. We'll give you ways to reflect on God's Word, internalize it, and ultimately start sharing it in ways you might not have considered before.

☐ **live it** This suggestion is usually for the more reflective among you. You want to share what God is doing, but you need to process what God is doing in *you* before you can share it with anyone else. The ideas here will help you do just that.

☐ **share it** You're already a relational person, and God built you that way. Therefore, you're ready to share Jesus with someone else in a meaningful way. So here's a way to do it. Now go make it happen!

☐ **go for it** You're probably a more creative or kinesthetic type. You want to share your faith, but you also want to do something a little more out-of-the-box. We've got just the thing for you. And here's where you'll find it.

☐ **do it together** Here are suggestions for something you can do together as a group. It might be an outreach event, a retreat, or just a great get-together outside your session time. Every so often, try one of these as a group, and see what God does with it.

By the way, if God has really spoken to you about something else during a session and you know you need to do whatever he's urging you to do, don't feel you have to choose from the ideas we've provided. Be obedient. Share what God is showing you with your group so they can pray for you and encourage you.

There's one more section to tell you about. It appears at the very end. It's not even part of the session per se, but it could end up meaning a lot to you.

Go Deeper

I can't emphasize this enough, so I'm repeating it: Discipleship is *not* about completing a curriculum. It's about developing and deepening the most important spiritual relationships you have—first with God, then with those God has brought you in contact with—because *none* of those relationships is an accident.

Therefore, it's possible you'll work through this season and think, Before I go any further, I *really* need a deeper understanding of... That's why we've provided a list of resources at the end of each session to help you do just that. At Group, we're not shy about recommending other publishers—and if a resource applies to more than one area of spiritual growth, we'll recommend it more than once. This isn't about selling Group products (although there's always much more dancing in the halls here when that happens). It's about your growing relationship with Jesus and about being willing to invite God into whatever you're still wrestling with.

And that painful thing you're feeling when you do that? That's called growth. But the good news is that we're in this together. So pull over whenever you need to! Or jump right into the next season. We're here for you either way.

Which brings us to a little reminder: If there's an area in which you'd like to see *us* dig deeper and create more resources to help *you*, tell us! Write to us at Group Publishing, Inc., P.O. Box 481, Loveland, CO 80539; or contact us via e-mail at smallgroupministry.com. We'd love to hear what you're thinking. (Yes—*really!*)

Choose Your Environment

Growing Out works well in a variety of venues. We want to help you wherever you are. Don't be shy about trying any of them! Here are some additional ideas, depending on your venue.

Sunday School

First, you may have noticed that I've chosen the word *group* instead of *class* throughout. Not every group is a class, but every class is a group. You're not here just to study and learn facts—you're also here to learn how to live out what you've learned. Together. As a group. We hope that becomes even truer as you work through these sessions.

We've constructed these sessions to run an hour at a brisk pace, but we understand the limitations a Sunday school program can put on the amount of time you spend on a session. So if a great question has started a great discussion and you don't want to cut it off, feel free to trim back elsewhere as needed. For example, since much of our field test group was made up of couples who could talk on the way home, we discovered that making "Walk It Out" a take-home instead of an in-class piece was one good way to buy back time without losing impact.

Try not to be one of those groups that say, "Great—we can skip that experience now!" Remember, the more senses and learning styles you engage, the more these sessions will stick. So play with these activities. Give yourself permission to fail—but go in expecting God to do the unexpected.

And if you don't have specific time limitations, read on.

Small Groups

If you need more than an hour for a session—and you're not tied to a clock or a calendar—take it! Again, taking the time to understand what God wants to tell your group is *way* more important than "covering the material" or staying within the one-hour or 13-week parameters. This happened repeatedly while field-testing—a great discussion ensued, people got down to things they were really wrestling with, and we decided we'd explore the session further the following week.

Learn to recognize rabbit trails—and get off them sooner rather than later—but don't short-circuit those occasions when the Holy Spirit is really working in people's lives. Those occasions will happen often in these sessions. If you're having a rich discussion and are really digging in, take an extra week and dig even deeper. Give the full meaning of the session time to sink in.

One-on-One Discipleship

Although this curriculum is designed for a larger group setting, we absolutely don't want to discourage you from using it in a more traditional, one-on-one discipleship setting. True, some of the activities might not work in a setting this small, and if that's the case, feel free to bypass them and go directly into the Bible passages and questions—there are plenty left to work with. The important thing is that you work together through the issues themselves, and at the pace that works for you.

But don't take this as an opportunity to entirely excuse yourselves from experiences—have a little fun together, and see what God does. Allow yourselves to be surprised.

Also—and it's probably obvious for this and the next scenario—all those recommendations we make to form smaller groups or twosomes? You can skip those and jump right into the discussion or activity.

Smaller Groups or Accountability Groups

One more thing: We don't want to discourage you from doing one-on-one discipleship, especially if you've already got a good thing going. There are some great and healthy mentoring relationships out there, and if you're already involved in one, keep at it! That said, research has shown repeatedly that learning can happen at a more accelerated rate—and more profoundly—in settings other than the traditional teacher-student relationship. So if you're just starting out, consider gathering in groups of three or four.

- A small group provides an environment that allows people to learn from one another. While there's often still a clear leader, the playing field feels more level, and the conversations often become more open and honest.

- If one person leaves for any reason—and there are plenty of legitimate ones—the group or accountability relationship isn't finished. Everyone else presses forward. No one is left hanging.

- The dynamics of a group of three or four are simpler than those of larger groups. And a group of three or four can be the best of both worlds, offering the rich discussions of a large group and the intimacy and accountability of one-on-one relationships.

- Again, we're about creating disciplers, and a smaller group allows growing disciplers to test-drive their own instructions, struggles, and transparency in an environment in which they can be both honestly critiqued and wholeheartedly encouraged. And when that happens, growth happens—for everyone.

If you'd like to delve into this further, Greg Ogden's *Transforming Discipleship* (InterVarsity) is a great resource to get you started, as are any number of materials from ChurchSmart Resources (churchsmart.com).

Whatever setting or environment you use for *Growing Out,* use it to its fullest. May God bless your efforts and those of the people with whom you share life!

Getting Connected

Pass your books around the room, and have people write their names, phone numbers, e-mail addresses, and birthdays in the spaces provided. Then make it a point to stay in touch during the week.

name	phone	e-mail	birthday

Who Are You— Really?

"*For we are God's masterpiece. He has created us anew in Christ Jesus, so we can do the good things he planned for us long ago*" (EPHESIANS 2:10).

In this session, we'll journey...

from ⎯⎯⎯⎯⎯⎯⎯⎯⟶ **to**
seeing where your faith already *is* your life...

understanding more deeply that God can use you wherever you are.

Before gathering, make sure you have...

○ pens or pencils for everyone

Optional activities (choose one or both):

○ **Option A:** The circle activity at the beginning of Go (see page 24)

○ **Option B:** DVD of *Chariots of Fire* (see page 29)

See **Leader Notes**, page 187.

Come and See

(about 15 minutes)

Before starting this first session, pass your books around the room, and have each person write his or her name, phone number, and e-mail address in the space provided on page 18.

》 Get into groups of three. Try to get with people you don't know well.

Give people time to group up.

》 Take a minute to tell the others in your group who you are and what you're about. When you're done, take up to another minute to discuss any questions others in your group might have before the next person shares.

There's one catch: You can't tell the others in your group what you do. No mention of jobs, hobbies, volunteer work—any kind of accomplishment or activity. So good luck. And go!

After six minutes, gather everyone back together, and discuss these questions:

> My purpose in life is simply to glorify God. We have to be careful that we don't let the pursuit of our life's goals, no matter how important they seem, cause us to lose sight of our purpose.
>
> —Tony Dungy,
> Quiet Strength

》 We're going to spend much of this season discovering how God has made each of us and what he has made each of us for. Before we go there, however, we're going to spend some time today realizing who we already are in Jesus.

As we come to understand who we are in Jesus more and more, his life can flow more easily from us into everything else we do—even when we're not consciously trying to serve him. So let's discover more about who we *really* are in Jesus.

◎ What are some things you *were* able to learn about each other?

◎ How does telling people what you do help them understand who you really are? How doesn't it?

◎ Let's have a re-do here: If you wanted people to know just one thing about you right now, what would it be?

Seek and Find

(about 25 minutes)

Have everyone get into groups of four or five.

》 Divide the following list of passages among you. Read them to yourselves first, and note what they say about who you are in Jesus. Once all of you are done, share about your passages with each other, and then discuss the questions that follow.

- John 15:15-16
- Romans 8:14-17
- Romans 8:31-39
- 2 Corinthians 5:16–6:2
- Ephesians 1:5-14
- Ephesians 2:4-10
- 1 Peter 2:9-10
- 2 Peter 1:3-4

Allow 15 minutes for discussion, and then come back together as a larger group and share highlights and insights from your discussion.

Seek and Find

 John 15:15-16; Romans 8:14-17; Romans 8:31-39; 2 Corinthians 5:16–6:2; Ephesians 1:5-14; Ephesians 2:4-10; 1 Peter 2:9-10; 2 Peter 1:3-4

◎ What encourages you about these verses?

◎ What is God telling you in these verses that you *still* have a hard time believing? Why?

◎ How does—or could—knowing who you are in Jesus affect every other part of your life? Give examples.

Go

(about 20 minutes)

If you've chosen to do **Option A**, *read on.*
If you're doing **Option B**, *go to page 29.*

» **Look at the illustration on your group page, and take a minute to answer the following to yourself: At what point in this circle do I no longer feel "safe" living out who I am in Jesus? Mark that place on the circle. What stops you from growing further?** ————————→

After people have marked their circles, ask for volunteers to share their answers.

> *If there's anything in life that we should be passionate about, it's the gospel... passionate in thinking about it, dwelling on it, rejoicing in it, allowing it to color the way we look at the world.*
>
> —C.J. Mahaney,
> The Cross
> Centered Life

» **I'm going to read a longer passage from Psalm 139. Close your eyes, and simply listen as I read. Think about what it says about you and God.**

Read Psalm 139:1-18, and then discuss these questions: ————→

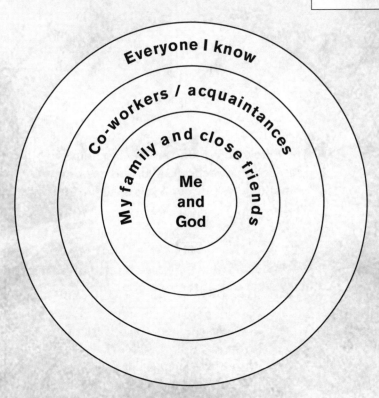

 Psalm 139:1-18

◎ How would believing that God really *is* everywhere help you to live out your faith?

◎ What—or who—could help you remember who you are in Jesus and help you stretch your circle of influence?

Walk It Out

(about 5 minutes)

> **》 The following options are here to help you put what you've learned into practice. But if God has prompted you to do something else through this session, then by all means do that!**

GROUP ▼

choose 1:

☐ know it

Set aside an hour this week—just you, God, and the Word. Review the Scripture passages from this session, and ask God to help you to see yourself the same way *he* sees you. (Don't worry about getting a big head— God can take of that, too, if he needs to.) As you discover how much God really loves and values you, take time to celebrate and thank God, and ask what you can do in response to his infinite love.

☐ live it

Get a piece of paper and draw seven columns—one for each day of the week. Along the left side, list the hours of the day, starting with the time you normally wake up and ending with the time you normally go to sleep. Now do your best to note your daily habits and routines in each column—what is your life normally like? Fill each hour of each day with a short description. Once you're done, *think about this:* When do you feel closest to God? Put a star by those times or days. When do you feel farthest or most distracted from God? Circle those times or days. Then look at your list. What does this tell you about when and how you experience God's presence? What might you do differently, so you can experience God in *every* part of your life?

☐ share it

Do you know someone who's truly living out his or her faith, maybe in areas of your life you haven't even imagined? Write that person a letter (or e-mail), and thank him or her for showing God's love to others.

Form pairs, select the option you'd like to take on this week, and share your choice with your partner. Write what you plan to do in the space provided, and make plans to connect with your partner before the next session to check in and encourage each other. Take five minutes to do that now.

☐ **go for it** Find a way to put your faith into action this week. Listen to someone who needs to talk. Love someone who is hurting. Give to someone who is in need. But don't do it just to do it; do it because of your faith in God—because you *want* to.

☐ **do it together**
As a group, decide on one way you can do good deeds *together*! Come alongside a church or civic organization; lead a clothing drive; help out in a soup kitchen—the choice is yours. Choose a time and place to get together this week and live out your faith.

...or think of your own!

Because I am God's wherever I go, I'll "Walk It Out" by:

_____

_____

_____

_____

_____

_____

Walk It Out continued

prayer⊙   Come back together as a group. Thank God for everything he's already done in your lives—and that *God* sees all of you as his masterpieces, whether *you* see yourselves that way or not. Ask God to show each person in your group that he really is with each of you everywhere you could possibly go. And ask God to help each of you see new ways of living out your lives in Jesus.

SEEING IT DIFFERENTLY
Go–Option B

LEADER To prompt your group to think about a session in a fresh way, we'll occasionally recommend video clips that your group can enjoy in place of (or in addition to) another part of the session. You'll be surprised by how effectively movies can portray eternal truths, or at least point toward them.

Instead of the circle activity, watch a scene from the movie *Chariots of Fire*. (If people need background: Eric Liddell was a celebrated Scottish runner and missionary. In this clip, he's trying to decide whether he should participate in the 1924 Olympics or go back to the mission field in China.) Cue the movie to 56:26 (DVD Chapter 20), as Eric is running up the stairs and the voice-over of Jennie is saying, "Training, training, training…." Stop the clip at 59:35, after Eric says, "To win is to honor him." Then discuss the following questions:

GROUP

◎ Do you normally look at "God's work" Jennie's way or Eric's? Explain.

◎ How much do you "feel [God's] pleasure" in your everyday life? Why do think that is (or isn't)?

Pick up at the reading of Psalm 139:1-18 on page 24.

Go Deeper

To dig deeper into understanding and walking out who we already are in Jesus, here are some great resources:

Discovering Your Identity in Christ by Charles F. Stanley (Thomas Nelson)

Outflow: Outward-Focused Living in a Self-Focused World by Steve Sjogren and Dave Ping (Group)

The Cross Centered Life: Keeping the Gospel the Main Thing by C.J. Mahaney with Kevin Meath (Multnomah)

Who I Am in Christ by Neil T. Anderson (Regal)

The Practice of the Presence of God by Brother Lawrence (Whitaker House)

Born to ~~Lead~~ Serve

But among you it will be different. Whoever wants to be a leader among you must be your servant, and whoever wants to be first among you must become your slave. For even the Son of Man came not to be served but to serve others and to give his life as a ransom for many" (MATTHEW 20:26-28).

In this session, we'll journey...

from ⟶ **to**
understanding what kind | discovering how to develop a
of ~~leaders~~ servants Jesus wants | deeper servant heart.
us to be...

Before gathering, make sure you have...

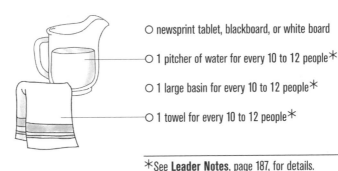

○ newsprint tablet, blackboard, or white board

○ 1 pitcher of water for every 10 to 12 people ✳

○ 1 large basin for every 10 to 12 people ✳

○ 1 towel for every 10 to 12 people ✳

✳See **Leader Notes**, page 187, for details.

Come and See

(about 10 minutes)

Ask everyone to get into pairs.

》 Think about a humbling or humiliating situation you've faced—for example, a layoff or demotion at work, something big you tried that failed in front of everyone, or even something embarrassing that happened when you were growing up. Share a little about it with your partner, and as you do, discuss these questions:

Allow five minutes for discussion, and then gather everyone back together to discuss highlights and insights.

》 Thank you for opening up to each other today. You just risked further humiliation and took a chance anyway—congratulations!

Today we're going to look at the topic of leadership and how Jesus led by example. And as we'll discover shortly, humility is a big key to understanding all of it. So let's begin to dig in.

One can so easily become too great to be used by God. One can never be too small for his service.

—Corrie ten Boom,
Not Good if
Detached

◎ Besides "humbled" or "humiliated," how else would you describe how you felt when this event was taking place?

◎ What good, if any, do you think came out of it?

Seek and Find

(about 30 minutes)

Ask for a volunteer or volunteers to read Philippians 2:3-11, 19-30.

>> The literal translation of the beginning of verse 7 is "he emptied himself." Jesus emptied himself. He gave up everything for us. Let's think about that a bit more, especially if this is the attitude God says each of us is supposed to have. ─────

> [T]hose chosen by our Lord to bear his message and carry on his work were for the most part 'uneducated and ordinary' people... The pattern seems to prove amply that in God's selecting them there would be no mistake as to the source of their words and authority.
>
> —Dallas Willard, Hearing God

>> Let's look at a very specific example of how our passage in Philippians played out in Jesus' life. Would someone please read John 13:1-17?

After your volunteer has read, say,

>> Now, I'd like all of you to take off your shoes and socks.

Once everyone's ready, discuss these questions: ─────

Philippians 2:3-11, 19-30

◎ What examples of Jesus' humility do you see in Timothy and Epaphroditus?

◎ How do you nonetheless see these two men as leaders? How do you see God (or Paul) honoring their attitude here?

◎ Do you think *we* need to be totally emptied of ourselves before God can really work through us? Why or why not?

◎ If you truly had "the same attitude that Christ Jesus had" (verse 5), what would be different about you?

 John 13:1-17

◎ Think about your family, those you work with, and even people you don't know very well. What are some realistic, practical ways that you can follow Jesus' example and serve them?

Seek and Find

If you have a chalkboard or white board, write down everyone's answers, thanking them for their responses. Then continue the discussion. ─────────────

After you've gotten some responses to that last question, discuss: ─────────────

》 **Serving others isn't always easy or comfortable, but Jesus showed us not only that we can do it but also that we can have joy *while* doing it. It can be hard to step out of our comfort zones, but everything Jesus did showed us that it's worth it to follow his example.**

◎ Out of all the ideas we've just shared, which ones do you think you would actually do? Explain.

◎ What's it been like wondering whether we would be washing each other's feet? Why?

◎ What makes you uncomfortable or unwilling to serve others? What can help you get past that?

Go

(about 20 minutes)

Ask for a volunteer to read Matthew 20:20–28.

(Just a reminder: Everyone's socks and shoes should still be off, and remain off until further notice.)

Discuss these questions: —————————————————

> 'The sea is the king of a hundred streams because it lies below them.' (quoting Lao Tzu) Jesus is like the sea because he serves all the people from the lowest depths although he himself is the king of all kings.
>
> —Joshua Choonmin Kang, Deep-Rooted in Christ

Matthew 20:20-28

◎ Be honest: In what ways are you like "the sons of Zebedee," James and John (or their mom, for that matter)?

◎ What's a situation right now where you would consider serving more fully…as long as it was on *your* terms?

◎ What would it take for you to let go of your "rights" and serve God however he wants you to serve—in that situation or any other?

Walk It Out

(about 5 minutes)

>> **The following options are here to help you put what you've learned into practice. But if God has prompted you to do something else through this session, then by all means do that!**

choose 1:

☐ know it

Memorize the text of Philippians 2:5-11, and set aside time each day to meditate on its meaning. Focus on the character of Jesus, praise him for his humility and amazing love, and invite the Holy Spirit to show you how you can respond to this passage in your daily life.

☐ live it

Take some time to pray about specific struggles with self that you face, such as self-centeredness, being preoccupied with your own goals rather than God's will, pride, a need to impress others, or a critical attitude toward others. Ask God to reveal one area you need to focus on. Invite a friend to pray for you as you seek to surrender this area of your life to God's control.

☐ share it

Get together for a meal with a Christian (or non-Christian) who is difficult to get along with. During the event or meal, focus on showing true humility. Set aside your own ambitions, goals, and preferences. Ask God to help you really love the person in front of you, and to open your heart to what God may be teaching you (and him or her) through your time together.

Form pairs, select the option you'd like to take on this week, and share your choice with your partner. Write what you plan to do in the space provided, and make plans to connect with your partner before the next session to check in and encourage each other. Take five minutes to do that now.

☐ **go for it** Follow Jesus' example by choosing a thankless, undesirable act of service you can do this week, such as scrubbing toilets (at home or at church), picking up trash in the park, scrubbing a friend's floors, or babysitting a neighbor's children. As you take on the task, remind yourself of Jesus' amazing example of humility.

☐ **do it together**

Plan a service opportunity in which your group can show Jesus' love and kindness to people living in difficult circumstances. Afterward, discuss as a group what God taught you during the experience. How did he enlarge your understanding of humility? What did God teach you about his love?

...or think of your own!

Because Jesus led by serving and wants us to do the same, I'll "Walk It Out" by:

_____

_____

_____

_____

_____

Walk It Out continued

Come back together as a group.

》 **Thank you for keeping your shoes and socks off all this time. I'd like to ask you to do one more thing, though— put all of your shoes in the middle of our group** [or bring them up front, depending on how your meeting area is set up]. **As you do, think of a way you've discussed or thought of today that you can "walk it out" and take the lead in serving someone else.**

Give people time to bring their shoes to your central location. You can either allow everyone to sit back down or gather in a circle—whichever you're more comfortable doing.

prayer⊖

》 **Let's pray. Jesus, thank you for not only giving us an example we can see and model ourselves after, but also for sending your Spirit so that we would have the power and ability to live out the things you put on our hearts. Help us to use both our hands and our feet to lead the way you want us to—by serving those around us. Give us not only your willingness but also your heart for the people you place around us. Amen.**

Go Deeper

To dig deeper into what servant leadership is and what it looks like, here are some great resources:

The Externally Focused Life by Rick Rusaw and Eric Swanson (Group)

Descending Into Greatness by Bill Hybels and Rob Wilkins (Zondervan)

The Servant Leader: Transforming Your Heart, Head, Hands, and Habits by Ken Blanchard and Phil Hodges (Thomas Nelson)

Servant Leadership: A Journey into the Nature of Legitimate Power and Greatness by Robert K. Greenleaf (Paulist)

Going to a Better Place...Together

We now have this light shining in our hearts, but we ourselves are like fragile clay jars containing this great treasure. This makes it clear that our great power is from God, not from ourselves" (2 CORINTHIANS 4:7).

In this session, we'll journey...

from ⟶ **to**

reflecting on how Jesus' example—and those of others— helps us to become more *like* Jesus...

committing to helping each other move forward in Jesus.

Before gathering, make sure you have...

○ No other supplies. Just *be* there!

Optional activities (choose one or both):

○ **Option A:** The pair-share that opens Come and See (see page 46)

○ **Option B:** DVD of *As Good as It Gets* (see page 54)

See **Leader Notes**, page 189.

Come and See

(about 10 minutes)

If you've chosen to do **Option A**, *read on.*
If you're doing **Option B**, *go to page 54.*

>> **Welcome! So far in this study we've discussed how God can use us where he's put us and how we can do what God asks us to do with more of a servant heart. So let's begin to pull all that together and move forward. Find a partner, and discuss these questions with him or her:** ——————————————→

> *Disciples do not just believe differently, they behave differently. They stick out. They provoke. They cause people to think. Disciples jar others to evaluate their own lives, often without uttering a word. Disciples point people to the kingdom of God simply by their behavior alone.*
>
> —Brian Jones,
> Getting Rid of the
> Gorilla

Come back together as a group (if you chose Option A), and share insights and highlights from your discussion time.

>> **Again, we've spent our first couple of sessions examining where God has put us and what kind of heart he wants us to have toward the people and situations he has put us with. In this session, we're going to begin to drill down a little deeper into specifics—what we can really do to become the hands, the feet, the heart of Jesus to those we encounter everywhere in our lives. And as we do that, we'll discover how can we help—and maybe even inspire—each other as members of the body of Christ.**

Come and See

◎ Who inspires you to be a better person?

◎ Is it because of his or her actions, because you want to make that person happy or proud...or *both*? or something else? Explain.

Seek and Find

(about 20 minutes)

Ask everyone to get into gender-specific groups of three. The reason for gender specificity will become clear in a few moments.

Have group members take turns reading 2 Corinthians 3:17–4:1, 2 Corinthians 4:6-11, and Hebrews 4:14-16, then discuss these questions: ⎯⎯⎯⎯⎯⎯⎯⎯⎯⟶

> *God has yet to bless anyone except where they actually are, and if we faithlessly discard situation after situation, moment after moment, as not being 'right,' we will simply have no place to receive his kingdom into our life. For those situations and moments are our life.*
>
> —Dallas Willard, The Divine Conspiracy

Allow 15 minutes for discussion. Gather people's attention, and ask them to stay with their groups. Share a few highlights and insights from your discussion time together.

》 God has allowed us to experience some incredible things—even if they may have seemed hard at the time—and God wants us to share with others what he's done and to give God the glory. There are probably also some things in our lives that we wish God hadn't allowed. But if we haven't already seen proof, God can and will use everything for his good, even those things that seem lousy and unexplainable to us—if we'll trust him.

2 Corinthians 3:17–4:1; 2 Corinthians 4:6-11; Hebrews 4:14-16

◎ Externally speaking, how do (or should) Jesus' and Paul's examples here inspire you to be more like Jesus?

◎ Internally speaking, how have you seen "the Spirit [make you] more and more like him" (2 Corinthians 3:18)? Give your *own* examples.

◎ When has God's light shone through you, despite your circumstances? How have those times changed the way you see God? yourself?

◎ On the other hand, when have you had a hard time seeing God at work? Why do you think God let you go through those circumstances anyway?

Go

(about 30 minutes)

>> As we've experienced God's glory, God has already equipped us to help others draw closer to him. Now we're going to start working out how we can help each other do that. Would someone please read Matthew 18:18-20?

> We must be ready to allow ourselves to be interrupted by God.
>
> —Dietrich Bonhoeffer, Life Together

After your volunteer has read, discuss:

Allow 10 minutes for discussion. Regain everyone's attention, and ask people to stay with their groups. Share a few highlights and insights from your discussion time together.

>> Earlier you shared about the people in your life who inspire you. Starting today, the group you're sitting with right now will help inspire you as well. From this point until we're done with this study, the people you're with will be *your* subgroup. The reason we want to keep gender-specific groups is to help everyone feel free to share honestly and feel as safe as possible.

Of course, the rest of the group is here for you as well, but the people you're with right now are the "others" you're going to spend time with to really dig into life together. And as we've just discussed, God brings people into our lives that we weren't expecting to help us grow. Right now, begin looking at the people you're with in that way. Learn from each other. Inspire each other. Pull each other up. And find ways to connect outside of our time here to do that as well. And then watch what God does with it.

Instead of our regular "Walk It Out" time today, share with each other your answers to these three questions. You might have answers to all three of them; you might not have answers for any of them right now. Either way, you're going to spend the next few months learning the answers together. Here are your three questions:

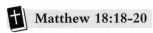 **Matthew 18:18-20**

◎ When has God unexpectedly brought one or two others into your life who helped you grow closer to Jesus? How did God use them?

◎ How does (or would) having other Christians you can trust in your life help you grow in Jesus in a way that going it alone can't?

◎ What things am I doing right now that God has clearly led me into—and how am I doing with them?

◎ What things might God be leading me to do now?

◎ What things might *stop* me from doing what God is leading me into?

Go continued

- **One: *What things am I doing right now that God has clearly led me into—and how am I doing with them?*** Has God been impressing you to be a better parent, a better spouse, a better steward of your time or resources? Has God called you to come out of a situation or a habit that's hurting you or others? Where has God put you? And how are you doing with it?

- **Two: *What things might God be leading me to do now?*** What do you think God's calling you to do right now? How has God been speaking to you lately? And what do you need to confirm that it really has been God prompting you?

- **And three: *What things might stop me from doing what God is leading me into?*** What's holding you back right now? Disobedience? Fear? Self-consciousness? Uncertainty? A lack of experience in an area you nonetheless feel God calling you into? What's holding you back from fulfilling God's will in your life right now?

The Lord does not ask if we have done well; He only examines if we have trusted in Him.

—Watchman Nee,

The Messenger of the Cross

After you've discussed your answers, take some time to pray for one another. Set aside a time during the week to touch base with one another, whether that's by phone, e-mail, texting, or seeing one another. Once you've done those things—discuss, pray, and decide how you're going to touch base during the week— you're free to go [or hang out, if you're in a small group].

May God bless you this week, and may he bless your new journey together!

Walk It Out

(about 5 minutes)

Because we're on this journey with God together, I'll "Walk It Out" by:

_____

_____

_____

_____

_____

_____

_____

_____

_____

_____

_____

_____

_____

SEEING IT DIFFERENTLY
Come and See–Option B

LEADER Instead of the pair-share in "Come and See," keep everyone together to watch a scene from the movie *As Good as It Gets.* Cue the movie to 1:39:11 (DVD Chapter 22), as Melvin says, "Now, I got a real great compliment for you…" Stop the clip at 1:41:15, as Melvin sighs in relief.

Keep everyone together, and pick up at the question, "Who inspires you to be a better person?" on page 47.

To dig further into how to share your walk with God with each other, here are some great resources:

In Pursuit of Jesus: Stepping Off the Beaten Path by Rick and Bev Lawrence (Group)

Experiencing God: Knowing and Doing the Will of God by Henry Blackaby, Richard Blackaby, and Claude King (B&H)

Doing Life Together DVD Curriculum: A Purpose Driven Group Resource by Brett Eastman, Dee Eastman, Todd Wendorff, Denise Wendorff, and Karen Lee-Thorp (Zondervan)

Simple Church: Returning to God's Process for Making Disciples by Thom S. Rainer and Eric Geiger (B&H)

Creating Community: Five Keys to Building a Small Group Culture by Andy Stanley and Bill Willits (Multnomah)

How God Made You—and Why

"*God works in different ways, but it is the same God who does the work in all of us. A spiritual gift is given to each of us so we can help each other*" (1 CORINTHIANS 12:6-7).

In this session, we'll journey...

from ———————————→ **to**
exploring what spiritual gifts are...

beginning to discover how God has gifted *you* to serve him and others.

Before gathering, make sure you have...

○ newsprint tablet, blackboard, or white board

○ a hefty snack with a variety of ingredients ✳

○ classical background music ✳

———————————
✳See **Leader Notes**, page 190, for details.

Come and See

(about 15 minutes)

>> **Welcome. Remember your groups from last week? (Good.) You're going to get back into them a little earlier than normal today, but since you're still getting used to each other, let's start with something easy. Grab a snack, and take two minutes to get back into your groups and discuss these questions:**

After two minutes, come back together as a larger group.

>> **Today we begin exploring spiritual gifts—what they are, who has them, and why God has given them to us. We had fun putting a few ingredients together; God brings together a lot of very different ingredients— us—to create something unique that can bring joy to others.**

We'll be exploring this from a variety of angles over the next several weeks so we can begin to understand how special God has created each of us—but to understand, too, that God didn't make us that way just so we could feel good about ourselves. God has a bigger plan, and we're all a part of it. God knows what we're ready for and wants each of us to know it, too. So let's start figuring out together what God has in mind for us.

> *If God hadn't put me on earth mainly to stroke tennis balls, he certainly hadn't put me here to be greedy. I wanted to make a difference, however small, in the world, and I wanted to do so in a useful and honorable way.*
>
> —Arthur Ashe

◎ Why did you choose that particular [food, topping, or filling]? Would you have eaten one of the other ones if that's all we had? Why or why not?

◎ Together, list all the ingredients you can think of that are in your snack. Which ingredients do we kind of take for granted, and why? Why is every ingredient important?

Seek and Find

(about 35 minutes)

Discuss: ————————————————————————

》 Let's begin to examine what God is referring to when the Bible talks about spiritual gifts and what they're all about.

Ask for volunteers to read 1 Corinthians 12:4-12 and 1 Peter 4:8-11. Then discuss: ————————————————————————

If you have a chalkboard or white board, write everyone's answers. Then continue your discussion: ————————————

Write these answers on your chalkboard or white board as well, if you have room. If people get stumped on coming up with ideas for a particular gift, it's OK to pass to the next one. Continue your discussion: ————————————————————

◉ When you hear the phrase "spiritual gifts," what comes to mind? Why *that* reaction?

 1 Corinthians 12:4-12; 1 Peter 4:8-11

◉ What spiritual gifts do you see mentioned in these two passages? Are there others not mentioned here? Which ones?

◉ How could you see each of these gifts being used, either in the church or outside it? Let's try to come up with an idea for each one.

◉ Some of these gifts look like things that even not-yet Christians could do, or arguably *have* done. So what would you say some of the differences are between a spiritual gift and a natural ability?

Seek and Find continued

Ask for another volunteer to read 1 Corinthians 12:14-27. ——

Write these answers on your chalkboard or white board as well, if you still have any room left.

》 While we haven't yet gotten into examining how God has specifically gifted each one of us, we probably already know a bit about how we're built. So let's discuss this question: ————

Seek and Find

 1 Corinthians 12:14-27

◎ Let's take this to another level. Look again at our list of gifts. What areas do you see where these gifts complement one another? Give some specific examples.

◎ Based on what you already know about yourself, which of the gifts we've listed make you say "*That's* not me"? How could someone who has that gift help you?

Go

(about 15 minutes)

》 Let's reflect one more time today on the idea that God has gifted each of you—and that he's done it for a reason. Get into your groups. Read the statement on your group page, and then discuss these questions: ———

Gather everyone's attention, keep them in their groups, and share highlights and insights from your discussions.

》 You've got a pretty big homework assignment this week. Everything here doesn't need to be completed this week, but as you'll be getting other assignments over the next several weeks that go with this, you'll want to get started as soon as possible. Therefore, we won't be doing an official "Walk It Out" section this week. We'll get back into that routine next week. Let's talk about your assignment.

At the end of this session is a series of forms, which you'll start on your own outside this group. The first one's the longest by far; it's your Spiritual Gifts survey. It'll probably take you about 30 to 40 minutes to complete. Answer all the questions truthfully and to the best of your knowledge, and then use the score sheet on page 70 to total your points. The categories that score the highest indicate what spiritual gifts you might be seeing in yourself.

But we have blind spots, too. That's where the sheets on pages 71 and 72 come in. The first, called "I See You..." is meant for you to give to others who know you well—preferably other Christians, in this case—so they can tell you how *they* see you. Make copies of this sheet for at least three people, so you get the most accurate feedback possible. If two people, or all of them, see the same things in you—especially if they

> When we see the holy purpose to which we are called, and then look upon ourselves, we too are utterly undone...To know as a fact that the work is too sacred for me to touch— that is the beginning of my usefulness.
>
> —Watchman Nee,
> Changed Into His Likeness

◎ Do you really believe this statement—that God could actually call *you* to do his work? Be honest, and explain your answer.

◎ In what ways does God's work *still* seem "too sacred for [you] to touch"?

◎ Do you see any places right now where God is tugging on your heart to get involved? What do you think—or wish—you could contribute to that situation?

know you well—that's a pretty good sign.

When you get all your responses back, tally them up on the "I See You..." score sheet. The responses just might surprise you. And if they do, ask God what he might be trying to show you.

And hang on to *everything*—we'll be putting it all together in a few weeks.

But for today, just spend a few minutes in your groups praying for one another. Ask God to begin to reveal to each member of your group the things he has called that person to. If there are other things you need to pray about together, by all means take the time to do that, too. Once you're done praying, you're free to go.

Go Deeper

To dig deeper into understanding spiritual gifts, here are some great resources:

Spiritual Gifts: 8 Studies for Individuals or Groups by R. Paul Stevens (InterVarsity)

S.H.A.P.E.: Finding and Fulfilling Your Unique Purpose for Life by Erik Rees (Zondervan)

Your Spiritual Gifts Can Help Your Church Grow by C. Peter Wagner (Regal)

Network: The Right People, in the Right Places, for the Right Reasons, at the Right Time by Bruce L. Bugbee, Don Cousins, and Wendy Seidman (Zondervan)

Unleash Your Church! by Paul Ford (ChurchSmart)

Spiritual Gifts Survey

Rate each of the statements as follows:

> **3 — Yep, that's me.**
>
> **2 — I'm like that pretty often.**
>
> **1 — I'm like that once in a while.**
>
> **0 — Are you kidding? Have you *met* me?**

Don't answer the following questions according to what you think *should be true or what you* hope *will be true in the future. Be honest and answer according to your current experience.*

When you're finished, score your survey using the spiritual gifts assessment sheet at the end.

---

1. _____ I like working out the plans for a situation or ministry, so everyone involved can be more organized and effective.

2. _____ I enjoy pursuing friendships with people who are different from me.

3. _____ I can often figure out what things others I'm mentoring or counseling are struggling with, even when they won't tell me.

4. _____ I enjoy encouraging and guiding those who are hurting or need direction.

5. _____ I regularly talk with my not-yet Christian friends about Jesus.

6. _____ I know God can accomplish the impossible, and I've seen him do it.

7. _____ I enjoy giving money to worthy causes.

8. _____ I've seen God miraculously heal people after I've prayed with them.

9. _____ I like taking routine tasks off other people's plates, so they can focus on more important things.

10. _____ I enjoy reaching out to people and making them feel accepted.

11. _____ Sometimes God stops me in my tracks and tells me to pray for a person or situation.

12. _____ God has shown me things that a person or group needed, even when I didn't fully understand the situation.

13. _____ When I take charge of a given situation, people tend to listen and follow.

14. _____ I enjoy helping the homeless or those struggling with poverty.

15. _____ I've seen growth in other people because I was willing to invest in them for an extended period of time.

16. _____ I feel that I'm being disobedient when I don't share a truth God has given me with others.

17. _____ When I see a task that needs to be done, I just take care of it.

18. _____ I especially enjoy studying and applying God's Word to my life.

19. _____ I'm very good at sensing what the Spirit wants for our church or in my life.

20. _____ I'm able to direct others who only see pieces of a given project.

21. _____ I would love to go overseas and help other Christians in their work.

22. _____ I can often tell when someone's struggling spiritually, even without knowing specific details about him or her.

23. _____ When others are in crisis, what I'm most concerned about is their spiritual condition.

24. _____ I don't compromise my faith with not-yet Christians, but I enjoy being with them and being a light to them.

25. _____ God has used me to fulfill visions that were way bigger than me, even though it was hard at times.

26. _____ I enjoy giving, but I prefer to give anonymously.

27. _____ People often seek me out for physical, emotional, or spiritual healing.

28. _____ I like working behind the scenes. In fact, I'd rather people *didn't* know what I do.

29. _____ I'm willing to open my home and provide for those in need.

30. _____ I have felt compelled to pray for people or situations without understanding why.

31. _____ I have recognized situations where the Spirit wanted to work, and I know those revelations didn't come from *me*.

32. _____ I enjoy rallying and leading others to advance Jesus and his church.

33. _____ People often call on me when someone they know needs help.

34. _____ I go out of my way to be available to those I encourage spiritually.

35. _____ God has led me to share biblical messages that applied directly to something either happening or about to happen.

36. _____ I like doing the little things that help build others up.

37. _____ I enjoy helping others grow in their knowledge of Jesus.

38. _____ When a topic is being discussed, I often can clarify what the real issues are.

39. _____ I am able to figure out and take the steps needed to resolve complex issues.

40. _____ I have a heart for people in other countries who need to hear the good news of Jesus.

41. _____ I can often sense when "something's not right" spiritually.

42. _____ I enjoy encouraging others with God's promises.

43. _____ I care a lot about people who don't know Jesus, and believe God uses me to reach them.

44. _____ I consistently believe God will fulfill his plans, even when it looks impossible.

45. _____ I strongly believe that some people, including myself, need to give sacrificially to advance God's work.

46. _____ I pray faithfully for people who need physical healing, whether I see healing or not.

47. _____ I often set aside my own plans so I can be available for others.

48. _____ My home isn't just for me and my family—it's a base camp for God's work.

49. _____ I seek prayer requests from others and consistently pray for them.

50. _____ I have often understood certain facts about people without actually being told them.

51. _____ I'm willing to step up when someone in the church needs to be disciplined.

52. _____ I'm always looking for ways to gather food and other necessities for people who struggle financially.

53. _____ I see caring for others as a marathon, not as a series of quick sprints.

54. _____ I've often received biblical insights about people and issues that I've needed to share.

55. _____ I'll take on a difficult task if I know it will help others and further God's kingdom.

56. _____ Others tell me they learn something new about God when I teach or lead a small group.

57. _____ I'm able to take spiritual truths and regularly apply them to my life.

58. _____ I'll do whatever it takes to meet a deadline we've agreed upon.

59. _____ I feel an unusual amount of compassion for people who are suffering in faraway places.

60. _____ When I look at a "spiritual" work, I can tell whether people are motivated by the flesh or whether they're really motivated by the Spirit.

61. _____ People are often encouraged to take positive steps after I've talked with them.

62. _____ God has used me to lead others to Jesus.

63. _____ I'm able to confidently trust in God despite difficulties, and I'm able to help others trust God, too.

64. _____ I enjoy sharing financial and material resources that help advance the good news of Jesus.

65. _____ I often sense that God is present and working to heal the person I'm praying for.

66. _____ I enjoy helping others when they're in need, and I do it often.

67. _____ I enjoy having guests, even when I'm not expecting them.

68. _____ I have often felt led to pray about something for an extended season.

69. _____ God has often given me unique insights into people's situations or problems.

70. _____ I get great satisfaction out of helping groups follow through on the plans they've committed to God.

71. _____ Helping others through a tough time helps me grow, too.

72. _____ Others often tell me that I've helped them grow closer to Jesus.

73. _____ The Spirit has often used me to provide spiritual guidance to others.

74. _____ I enjoy being available to help others, inside or outside the church.

75. _____ I regularly share biblical truths in a way that helps others.

76. _____ I've had spiritual insights that helped resolve issues between others.

77. _____ People ask for my advice when they're trying to put a plan together.

78. _____ I want unreached people to *get* reached, so they can know Jesus, too.

79. _____ Others have told me that I can "sense" the motives in a person's heart.

80. _____ I can see God working in other people's lives, even when those people can't.

81. _____ I am able to share about Jesus in a way that not-yet Christians "get it."

82. _____ Once I've committed something to God in prayer, I expect God to answer it.

83. _____ I know God will meet my needs, no matter *how* much I give.

84. _____ It makes me happy when God uses me to help bring healing to others.

85. _____ I prefer short-term tasks to long-term commitments.

86. _____ Others have told me that I make them feel welcome and accepted.

87. _____ I often sense the Spirit actively helping me to pray.

88. _____ I can tell when thoughts or impressions are from the Spirit and when they're just coming from me.

89. _____ When I'm in a group, I usually wind up being the leader.

90. _____ I not only feel deeply for those who are suffering, but I do something about it.

91. _____ I love helping others grow in their spiritual walks.

92. _____ I don't see doctrine as a barrier between people, but as a way to help them understand who God is.

93. _____ I'm more task-oriented than people-oriented.

94. _____ I get great satisfaction from helping others learn what God's taught me.

95. _____ People think I have a lot of wisdom, even if I'm not the most educated person in the room.

Spiritual Gifts Survey Score Sheet

Spiritual Gifts Score Sheet					Total	Spiritual Gift
1	20	39	58	77		Administration
2	21	40	59	78		Apostleship
3	22	41	60	79		Discernment
4	23	42	61	80		Encouragement
5	24	43	62	81		Evangelism
6	25	44	63	82		Faith
7	26	45	64	83		Giving
8	27	46	65	84		Healing
9	28	47	66	85		Helping
10	29	48	67	86		Hospitality
11	30	49	68	87		Intercession
12	31	50	69	88		Knowledge
13	32	51	70	89		Leadership
14	33	52	71	90		Mercy
15	34	53	72	91		Pastoring
16	35	54	73	92		Prophecy
17	36	55	74	93		Service
18	37	56	75	94		Teaching
19	38	57	76	95		Wisdom

I See You...

Find at least three people who know you well, and give each of them a copy of this page. Ask them to first circle the 5 words or phrases from the list that best describe you, then rate those descriptions from 1 to 5, 1 being the description that best captures who they think you are. Have them return their sheets to you when completed.

This is how I see _____

Planner	Organizer	Detail-oriented
"Starter"	"Spiritual pioneer"	Goes wherever God leads
Distinguishes flesh from spirit	Sees what's *really* going on	Senses when "something's off"
Helps people keep going	Motivator	Encourages next steps
Shares faith anywhere	Leads others to Jesus	Loves to talk about Jesus
Believes God's promises	Steps out in faith	"God finishes what he starts"
Charitable	Shares what he/she has	Generous
Brings wholeness	Healer	Restores others to health
Always lends a hand	Does "the little things"	Works behind the scenes
Accepts others	Provides a "safe place"	Puts people at ease
Prayer warrior	Prays for others–a lot	Gets answers to prayer
Knows what God wants now	Has God-given insight	Gets "words from God"
Makes things happen	Gives practical guidance	Sees the big picture
Helps the helpless	Compassionate	Comforts the suffering
Guides spiritually	Cares for/grows others	People-sensitive
Speaks boldly	Speaks God-given truth	Biblically "far-sighted"
Sees needs and meets them	Helps wherever, whenever	Jumps in where needed
Communicates truth clearly	Helps others "get it"	Makes the Bible "real"
Perceptive	Applies knowledge	Has "practical faith"

Signed: _____

"I See You..." Score Sheet

Note the addition of the gifts in the far left column. Tally everyone's 5 circled choices, noting the rating each person gave (from 1 to 5).

Administration	Planner	Organizer	Detail-oriented
Apostleship	"Starter"	"Spiritual pioneer"	Goes wherever God leads
Discernment	Distinguishes flesh from spirit	Sees what's really going on	Senses when "something's off"
Encouragement	Helps people keep going	Motivator	Encourages next steps
Evangelism	Shares faith anywhere	Leads others to Jesus	Loves to talk about Jesus
Faith	Believes God's promises	Steps out in faith	"God finishes what he starts"
Giving	Charitable	Shares what he/she has	Generous
Healing	Brings wholeness	Healer	Restores others to health
Helps	Always lends a hand	Does "the little things"	Works behind the scenes
Hospitality	Accepts others	Provides a "safe place"	Puts people at ease
Intercession	Prayer warrior	Prays for others–a lot	Gets answers to prayer
Knowledge	Knows what God wants now	Has God-given insight	Gets "words from God"
Leadership	Makes things happen	Gives practical guidance	Sees the big picture
Mercy	Helps the helpless	Compassionate	Comforts the suffering
Pastoring	Guides spiritually	Cares for/grows others	People-sensitive
Prophecy	Speaks boldly	Speaks God-given truth	Biblically "far-sighted"
Service	Sees needs and meets them	Helps wherever, whenever	Jumps in where needed
Teaching	Communicates truth clearly	Helps others "get it"	Makes the Bible "real"
Wisdom	Perceptive	Applies knowledge	Has "practical faith"

Experience Is the Best Teacher

And we know that God causes everything to work together for the good of those who love God and are called according to his purpose for them" (ROMANS 8:28).

In this session, we'll journey...

from ⟶ **to**
examining how God has already grown us through our experiences...

understanding what God might be preparing us *for*.

Before gathering, make sure you have...

○ pens or pencils for everyone

Optional activities (choose one or both):

○ **Option A:** The activity at the beginning of Go (see page 81)

 ○ 1 small (roughly 2-inch and preferably smooth) stone for each person. If you're short of time, any small rock will work.

 ○ 1 permanent marker for each group

 ○ **Option B:** DVD of *The Wizard of Oz* (see page 85)

See **Leader Notes**, page 192.

Come and See

(about 10 minutes)

Have everyone get into their groups and discuss these questions: ─────────────────────────

Allow five minutes for discussion. Bring everyone back together, and share highlights and insights from your discussion time.

Ask for someone to read Ephesians 2:10.

》 Today we're going to spend time with another set of teachers—God, and the experiences God uses to prepare us for good works. When we look back on our lives, it's not always easy to figure out how we got here—or to believe that God could use what we've been through, let alone the things we've done to ourselves. But God knows every experience we've ever had—everything we've accomplished, everything we've learned, everything we've suffered through, every stupid mistake we wish we could take back— far better than we do. God is still creating us, in the sense that he's shaping each of us into the people he wants us to be. And God wants to use everything in us to create something special, in our lives and in every life we come in contact with.

So let's begin to discover together how God has been preparing us all along and what he might be preparing us for.

Come and See

◎ Who's the best teacher you've ever had—whether it was at school or somewhere else? In what ways did he or she positively impact your life?

◎ When have you found yourself in the role of teacher? What did you find rewarding or unrewarding about it?

◎ What do you enjoy more, learning from others or teaching them? Why?

Seek and Find

(about 35 minutes)

Ask for volunteers to read Romans 8:28-32 and Philippians 1:6-11. Then discuss:

》 **Let's look further at what God might want to use—and what he's already used—in our own lives. Get back into your groups.**

Give groups time to reassemble. Make sure everyone has a pen or pencil.

> *We do not have to get up into some exalted state to find Christ, or down into some profound and terrible experience. We can find Him everywhere we are...We can take Him as we are, and He will lead us into all the experiences we need.*
>
> —A.B. Simpson,
> The Fourfold
> Gospel

》 **We're going to spend some time reflecting on the times and places God has met us throughout our lives. We've just discussed one situation in our lives like that. Even if you didn't share it, you probably thought of one. There probably have been others, too. It may have been a mountaintop experience when you knew God was doing incredible things and you were in the middle of it. It might have been a time you were in the valley, but God was still especially close. It may have been a time you didn't even know God was working through, but looking back you can clearly see what God was up to.**

Look at page 78. On your own, read the questions, and think about when God has been especially present in your life. Write your answers as they come to you. Once you've spent about five minutes thinking the questions through, list those moments on page 79 in the order they happened. There are 10 lines—use as many or as few as you need. Then look over your list and try to answer the questions on page 79. If you don't have answers right now, that's OK, but start thinking about them.

Use about 15 minutes to work through these pages on your own, and then take another 10 minutes to share your answers with your group. Then let's come back together.

Romans 8:28-32; Philippians 1:6-11

◎ Why is "loving God" so important in this passage?

◎ Why do we need both love *and* knowledge to become more like Jesus?

◎ Think about a time God turned a bad situation into something good because you loved and trusted him. What did God teach you from the experience? How did God use it to make you at least a little bit more like Jesus?

Seek and Find continued

God's Work in Progress

Think about it:

- When have you taken a big step of faith or obedience because you knew it was what God wanted?

- When have you been conscious of God guiding your steps, whether you knew it at the time or realized it later on?

- When have you felt most fulfilled in your walk with Jesus? What was taking place in your life at the time?

Reflect on it:

1. _____

2. _____

3. _____

4. _____

5. _____

6. _____

7. _____

8. _____

9. _____

10. _____

• What patterns, if any, do you see in situations God has put you in?

• Based on what you've written—or even if it's *not* based on what you've written—where do you think God might be trying to take you next?

Seek and Find continued

Allow 25 minutes for groups to reflect and discuss, and then gather everyone's attention, keeping them with their groups.

prayer⊙

》 **God has done incredible things in our lives. So before we go any further here, let's pause a minute and thank him for that.** (Pause.)

Lord, we thank you for everything you bring into our lives—for things that have fulfilled the desires of our hearts as well as yours, for ways you've let us help you even when you could have done it all yourself, even for things that may have been painful at the time but have helped others see your glory. Help us to see where you want us to be next—the tasks, the relationships, the ways we need to be with you so you can prepare us. In Jesus' name, amen.

Pause a few moments.

》 **We've already spent a chunk of time exploring how God has used our experiences both to shape us and to reveal how he's uniquely built each of us. If you haven't already started your Spiritual Gifts survey and given your "I See You..." pages from last week to your friends, here's a reminder to do that. You've probably discovered some things about yourself today, but God wants to show you even more, and to use what he shows you—use *you*—to reveal his life in you to every person God puts you in contact with.**

Go

(about 15 minutes)

If you've chosen to do **Option A**, *read on.*
If you're doing **Option B**, *go to page 85.*

Give a stone to everyone and a marker to each group.

》 Let's look once more at the page you've worked through together. Look at your closing questions again, and think about your answers. On the stones you've each been given, take turns writing down a word or phrase that sums up where you think God is pointing next. Again, if you don't have an answer yet, that's OK—draw a blank line on your stone, and spend time this week praying that God will show you how he wants to fill in that space.

Take your rock with you when you leave. Keep it as a reminder of how God is guiding you even now. Each time you look at it, ask God to reveal even more of what he wants to do.

When you're done, go on together to "Walk It Out," and discuss what each of you will do in response to what God has shown you this week. Let's come back together in 10 minutes.

Walk It Out

(about 5 minutes)

》 The following options are here to help you put what you've learned into practice. But if God has prompted you to do something else through this session, then by all means do that!

choose 1:

☐ know it

Spend some time in Psalms this week. It's full of experiences, praises, pain, celebration, confusion, and the ability to see where God's been working (and to praise God even when the psalmist *can't* see the good in the moment). Try to read at least five psalms a day this week—and if God speaks to you through your reading, keep it going and finish all 150 psalms in a month.

☐ live it

Spend some more time thinking through and reflecting on your "God's Work in Progress" page. There's a good chance that other times you've encountered God didn't immediately come to mind today. Add them to your page. Take time to reflect on what God has been doing and what he might want to do next. Spend time thanking God for your past, your present, *and* your future.

☐ share it

If there's someone God has particularly put on your heart—especially if that person's represented on your stone—give your stone to that person as you share what God has been showing you. Use this opportunity to say how much this person really matters to you and—what's even more important—to God.

Form pairs, select the option you'd like to take on this week, and share your choice with your partner. Write what you plan to do in the space provided, and make plans to connect with your partner before the next session to check in and encourage each other. Take five minutes to do that now.

☐ **go for it** Use your blessings to bless others. Think of a way you can share God's abundance in your life with someone you don't know well—or at all. It might be something as small as calling with a word of encouragement or giving a plate of cookies, or as large as making a rent payment for a single mom who's struggling to make ends meet.

☐ **do it together**

With your (larger or smaller) group, work to gather food or clothing for the needy in your community. But this time, change it up a bit. Think about it: What has God given to you that's been a blessing to *you,* either individually or as a group? Instead of cans of pork and beans or used clothing, give away something precious to you. Let your sacrifice really *be* a sacrifice. And make it a joyful sacrifice. Distribute the items yourselves if you have an outlet for them, or use an existing organization such as The Salvation Army.

...or think of your own!

Because God's been preparing me all along to do his will, I'll "Walk It Out" by:

_____

_____

_____

_____

Walk It Out continued

prayer⊙

Come back together as a group. If you did the stone activity, ask people to hold their stones in front of them as you lead them in prayer.

》 Lord, again we thank you for those times you've been especially visible in our lives, for all the experiences you've used to shape our lives, and for all the ways you want to become even more visible through our lives. Thank you for the people you've put in our lives and on our hearts. Help us to see how we can show your love to them even more.

We thank you in advance for the incredible things you're going to do through us. In Jesus' name, amen.

SEEING IT DIFFERENTLY

Go—Option B

LEADER   Instead of the stone activity in "Go," keep everyone together to watch a scene from *The Wizard of Oz*. Cue the movie to 1:27:30 (DVD Chapter 48), as Dorothy and friends approach the Wizard. Stop the clip at 1:32:18, after Dorothy says, "Oh, they're all wonderful."

Get into your groups, and discuss the following questions. Most of you are probably familiar with this movie, so if other scenes come to mind as we discuss, feel free to bring them up.

GROUP

◎ When have you felt like "that man [or woman] behind the curtain"—like you were projecting an image you couldn't live up to?

◎ In what ways was the Wizard not such a "humbug" after all? How did he keep his promises to the Scarecrow, the Cowardly Lion, and the Tin Man?

◎ Who or what would help you see more clearly how God has already been working in you and what he might want to do next? How will you follow up on that this week?

Have everyone get back into their groups and go to "Walk It Out." It starts on page 82.

Go Deeper

To discover more about what God has already done in your lives and what he might want to do next, here are some great resources:

God Is Closer Than You Think: This Can Be the Greatest Moment of Your Life Because This Moment Is the Place Where You Can Meet God by John Ortberg (Zondervan)

Discovering God's Will: How to Know When You Are Heading in the Right Direction by Andy Stanley (Multnomah)

Experiencing God: Knowing and Doing the Will of God by Henry Blackaby, Richard Blackaby, and Claude King (B&H)

Hearing God: Developing a Conversational Relationship With God by Dallas Willard (InterVarsity)

Letting God Unwrap Your Gifts

And so, dear brothers and sisters, I plead with you to give your bodies to God because of all he has done for you. Let them be a living and holy sacrifice—the kind he will find acceptable. This is truly the way to worship him. Don't copy the behavior and customs of this world, but let God transform you into a new person by changing the way you think. Then you will learn to know God's will for you, which is good and pleasing and perfect" (ROMANS 12:1-2).

In this session, we'll journey...

from ─────────────→ **to**

reflecting on the gifts, talents, passions, and desires God has given us...

discovering how to let God use them the way *he* wants them used.

Before gathering, make sure you have...

Optional activities (choose one or both):

○ **Option A:** Discuss Hebrews 6 at the end of Seek and Find (see page 90)

○ **Option B:** DVD of *Walk the Line* (see page 97)

See **Leader Notes**, page 192.

Come and See

(about 10 minutes)

Have people get into their groups and discuss these questions:

Come back together, and share highlights and insights from your group discussions.

》 Some of us have known what we wanted to be since we were very young. For most of us, however, our dreams have been changed over the years, maybe even much later in life than we expected. And for many of us, coming to know Jesus changed our dreams, too. As we've turned our lives over to God, the Spirit has given us new desires and dreams. Some we may already be putting into practice, others we're still figuring out, and others the Spirit has yet to reveal to us because God knows we're not ready.

We'll spend time today on those last two. We're going to pick up from last week—what are the next steps God might be preparing us for?—and examine what God needs to change in us first so these things can happen. Then we'll look at how we can help clear the way for God to do that.

If we get to thinking that it is our best assets that make us most valued to the Lord, we are close to being useless. We must become acquainted with our weaknesses if we are to see him use us for great purposes.

—Neil Cole,
Search & Rescue

Come and See

◎ What was the one thing you most wanted to do or be when you grew up?

◎ How did that dream either grow stronger, change, or fall away as you got older?

◎ What's one dream you have right now—no matter how far-fetched— that you'd like to accomplish someday?

Seek and Find

(about 30 minutes)

Ask for a volunteer to read Romans 12:1-8. Then discuss: ——

Have another volunteer read 2 Corinthians 3:4-6. Then
discuss: ——————————————————————————————————→

If you've chosen to do **Option A**, *read on.*
If you're doing **Option B**, *go to page 97.*

Have another volunteer read Hebrews 6:10-16. Then discuss: ——

Seek and Find

 Romans 12:1-8

◎ Practically speaking, what does it mean to be a "living and holy sacrifice"? How does it enable us to know God's "good and pleasing and perfect" will—and actually *do* it?

◎ Look at verses 4 through 8 again. How does having a sacrificial attitude help us deal with those who are built different from us? Give examples.

 2 Corinthians 3:4-6

◎ How does it help you to know that it's *God* who makes us "qualified"? What, if anything, bugs you about that idea?

◎ Does that mean we do nothing and just wait until God is ready to give us our next task? Explain.

 Hebrews 6:10-18

◎ What things do you do in your daily life—materially, spiritually, or both—just because "they need to get done," and why?

◎ For each thing you've mentioned, do you need to stop doing it, change the way you do it, or just change the attitude you do it with? Explain.

Go

(about 20 minutes)

Have people get into their groups, read the quote on the group page, and discuss these questions:

Allow 10 minutes for discussion, and then gather everyone's attention, keeping them in their groups. Ask for groups to share highlights and insights from their discussion time.

》 Next week we're going to start putting everything together—our gifts, our talents, our passions—and discover together what God might be wanting next for each of us. So be sure to bring all the forms you've worked on the past couple weeks. Make sure you've worked through your score sheets *before* you come next week.

After this session is a description of each of the spiritual gifts covered in your surveys. At the very least, read over the gifts that are showing up in *your* surveys. Better yet, read all of them. There may be something all of you have missed, and you'll have a greater appreciation for how God has built each person and the ability to recognize it in them.

Anyway, we're going to do some serious work together next week, and as we do that work, God will honor it and begin to show us things in ourselves that we've never seen—even though he's seen them in us all along.

Now go on to "Walk It Out." Take five minutes to decide on what options you'll take on, take a few minutes to pray for each other, and then let's come back to pray together.

> *The trick to uncovering people's values is to assess how they invest their time, energy, money, and passion...Ideals are what you want; values are what you do. Ideals become values only if they are lived out.*
>
> —Mark Driscoll,
> The Radical Reformission

◎ What's something you know God has gifted you with—again, spiritually, materially, or both—that you wish God would tell you how to use?

◎ If there were one thing at all you could do for God right now, and you knew for sure it would work, what would it be?

◎ Be honest then: Why aren't you already doing it?

◎ What do you need to grab hold of—or let go of—so God can turn your ideals into values?

Walk It Out

(about 5 minutes)

》 The following options are here to help you put what you've learned into practice. But if God has prompted you to do something else through this session, then by all means do that!

GROUP ▼

choose 1:

☐ **know it**
Spend 15 minutes each day this week meditating on Romans 12:1-2. What does God want to transform in *your* life? What's God calling you to sacrifice? Spend time handing that thing over to God each day this week, and see what God places in those newly opened hands instead.

☐ **live it** Spend time with a Christian friend. Ask this person to be totally candid with you about both the good things he or she sees in you as well as the areas you really haven't fully given over to God. You could even do the same for that person, if he or she is willing. Either way, make a point of praying together when you're done, for everything that's been brought up.

☐ **share it** Take a step out of your comfort zone. Reach out to a non-Christian friend or co-worker who needs help. Don't go with an attitude of "*now* they'll see Jesus." Hopefully they will, but don't look at it that way. Use what God has given you. Let God use it however *he* wants to.

Form pairs, select the option you'd like to take on this week, and share your choice with your partner. Write what you plan to do in the space provided, and make plans to connect with your partner before the next session to check in and encourage each other. Take five minutes to do that now.

☐ **go for it** What ideal or dream have you been talking about—and doing nothing about—for way too long? Address it this week. Figure out who you need to talk to, or what other actions you need to take, and begin to make it happen this week. Don't go in expecting you have to know everything—or maybe even *anything*—but expect that as you move forward, God will honor your steps of faith and guide you in the way you need to go.

☐ **do it together**
Perhaps as you've discussed your dreams, ideals, and gifts together, you've spotted a common thread. Address it. How can you serve together in a way that highlights your gifts and passions without showing them off? If God is putting something on your hearts, and you feel you've got nothing in your heads, don't let it stop you. Find someone who can come alongside you to teach you or who can advise you on how to get started. Then do it!

...or think of your own!

Because I want God to use my gifts, talents, passions, and desires the way *he* wants them used, I'll "Walk It Out" by:

_____

_____

_____

Walk It Out continued

prayer⊙

Come back together as a group. Thank God for everything he's been revealing to your group over the last several weeks. Ask God to help each of you see those things more clearly, as well as what you're each still holding back, whether you've done it intentionally or not. Close by asking God for the wisdom and courage to take the next steps he wants each of you to take.

Remind everyone to bring books and all other forms they've been working on ("Spiritual Gifts" survey and score sheet and "I See You..." pages and score sheet) next week.

Go Deeper

To dig deeper into the importance of dedicating our gifts, talents, and dreams—and our fears about them—to God, here are some great resources:

The Externally Focused Life by Rick Rusaw and Eric Swanson (Group)

Do Hard Things: A Teenage Rebellion Against Low Expectations by Alex Harris and Brett Harris (Multnomah)

The Church of Irresistible Influence: Bridge-Building Stories to Help Reach Your Community by Robert Lewis and Rob Wilkins (Zondervan)

The Radical Reformission: Reaching Out Without Selling Out by Mark Driscoll (Zondervan)

SEEING IT DIFFERENTLY
Seek and Find–Option B

LEADER   Instead of the reading and discussion of Hebrews 6, watch a scene from the movie *Walk the Line.* Cue the movie to 23:48 (DVD Chapter 8), as Johnny and his band begin playing. Stop the clip at 29:41, as Johnny and Vivian hug. (If you choose to read Hebrews anyway, do this segment afterward.)

GROUP

◎ What different emotions do you see Johnny go through during this scene?

◎ In one sense, Johnny was using his gift throughout this scene, but something changed. What was it, and what helped it to change?

◎ "All right, let's bring it home": Why is it easier to play "that same…tune"—at your job, with your friends, in your church, wherever—than to do "something different...something real"?

◎ What are the rewards to discovering and singing *your* "one song"? What are the risks? And in each case, what might that look like?

Pick up at "Go." It starts on page 92.

Spiritual Gifts

What They Look Like and What to Look Out For

Administration

The God-given ability to understand how an organization or ministry functions, and the ability to design and carry out a plan of action that accomplishes those goals

◎ **What It Looks Like**

Turning visions into realities

Fleshing out the details and coming up with workable plans

Helping ministries become more effective and efficient

Focusing on the details rather than the big picture

Putting the pieces together, and telling people how to follow through

◎ **What to Look Out For**

Viewing people as "a means to an end"

Becoming inflexible about adjusting plans

Not fully communicating expectations—or praise—to team members

Relying on the plan instead of the Spirit and prayer

Favoring those who "stick to the plan"

Apostleship

The divine enablement to start and oversee new churches or large-scale ministries

◎ **What It Looks Like**

Literally being "on a mission"

Creating the foundations that enable churches and ministries

Adapting to other cultures and settings easily

Overseeing a group of churches or ministries, helping develop leadership

What to Look Out For

Having a problem letting go of "my baby"

Operating in the flesh and calling it the Spirit

Wanting to move on to the next big thing before the current work is strong enough to function on its own

Demanding more than others are capable of giving

Discernment

The capability to distinguish between truth and error, or right and wrong, and to recognize whether motives or actions have their source in God, flesh, or Satan

What It Looks Like

Readily sensing when spiritual warfare is taking place

Often seeing or sensing spiritual issues before others do

Helping to uncover the spiritual source of a practical, physical, or emotional problem

Ability to see when others are being deceived

What to Look Out For

A tendency to "see Satan under every rock"

A tendency to become judgmental of others

Being overly blunt with others, rather than lovingly revealing the truth

Disregarding practical changes people can make to address their problems

Encouragement

The ability to strengthen others by God's truth, or to comfort or urge them to action when they're discouraged or doubtful

What It Looks Like

Coming alongside those who are discouraged

Gently pushing others not just to learn God's Word but to apply it

Telling the truth and, at the same time, helping others feel lifted up—even when the truth hurts

Being more of an on-the-spot encourager than a long-term counselor or pastor

◎ What to Look Out For

Not following through due to wanting to encourage the next person

Jumping to conclusions before knowing the full story

Choosing to keep things positive rather than confront them, even when confrontation is needed

Focusing more on the practical steps a person needs to take than on the actual person

Evangelism

The ability to effectively communicate the good news of Jesus to non-Christians in a way that they hear and follow Jesus, too

◎ What It Looks Like

Wanting to share Jesus with everyone—even strangers

Showing not-yet Christians who Jesus really is, and doing it in such a way that they're drawn to God

Wanting everyone to be able to share their faith

Sharing God's passion to bring everyone to Jesus

◎ What to Look Out For

Being pushy or obnoxious if trying to bring others to Jesus on their own strength

Playing "the numbers game" regarding how many people they've led to Jesus

Using guilt to motivate others to share their faith

Not following up with people after leading them to Jesus

Not recognizing need to rely on the Spirit rather than on personal abilities to bring others to Jesus

Faith

The divinely inspired confidence and unwavering belief in God's ability to fulfill his purposes

◎ **What It Looks Like**

Consistently trusting God to fulfill his promises, supernaturally if necessary

Being confident that everything works for God's glory, no matter how difficult or lousy things might appear

Willingness to do God's will no matter what and no matter who comes along (or doesn't)

Believing God's promises, and enabling other people to do the same

Believing God will deliver whatever is needed when it's needed

◎ **What to Look Out For**

Losing patience with people's fear or caution

Mistaking personal vision for God's vision, thus setting themselves or others up for frustration or failure

Being stubborn and unwilling to listen to others' advice

Seeing others' concerns as criticism of God—or of what God has revealed to them—rather than an opportunity to clarify God's vision to them

Giving

The divine enablement to give freely and sacrificially of one's time and resources for the sake of Jesus and his church

◎ **What It Looks Like**

Freely and sacrificially giving whatever they have, whenever it's needed

Seeing the possessions God has given them as opportunities for service

Consciously making lifestyles adjustments in order to give as much as possible

Giving discreetly, without making a show of it

Supporting people and causes passionately

What to Look Out For

Giving at the family's expense

Being critical of the way others use their money and resources

Give without checking sufficiently into how money is used

Thinking that giving entitles them to a bigger say in how things are done

Healing

The divine ability to restore people to wholeness through a direct of act of God (emotional, relational, spiritual, physical, etc.)

What It Looks Like

Believing that God can heal anyone in any situation—and has played a role when healing happens

Willingness to pray for anyone who asks for healing, even when it seems impossible

Willingness to pray long-term for healing, as God gives them the faith to do so

Using the healing gift to confirm a message from God

What to Look Out For

Being overly proud or feeling entitled because of this gift

Taking responsibililty for healing, instead of giving God the glory

Feeling responsible for someone *not* being healed, rather than seeing it as God's sovereign decision

Helping

The divine enablement to accomplish practical and necessary tasks which free up, support, and meet the needs of others

What It Looks Like

Taking pleasure in serving God through everyday responsibilities

Seeing what needs to be done and wanting to help, even with a small task

Being unselfish in nature

Taking the "little things" off other people's plates so they can use their gifts

Seeing practical actions as spiritual ones

◎ What to Look Out For

Thinking "I don't do anything special"

Getting stretched past the ability to be useful because of inability to say no

Feeling taken for granted if no one recognizes their contribution

Not allowing other potential helpers to share the load

Neglecting their own families in order to help others

Hospitality

The divine enablement to care for people by providing fellowship, food, or shelter

◎ What It Looks Like

Creating a caring environment

Helping others feel welcome

Providing a "safe place" where relationships can develop

Liking to connect people who didn't previously know each other

◎ What to Look Out For

Not doing more than just entertain guests

Not knowing who God wants them to reach out to

Obsessing about appearances before entertaining company

Intercession

The supernatural ability to pray extensively and fervently for others, seeing frequent and specific results

◎ What It Looks Like

Desiring to pray intensely for other people or causes

Being intensely aware of the spiritual battles being fought during prayer

Being convinced that God responds promptly to prayer

Responding to the Spirit's leading in prayer, whether or not it makes sense at first

Equipping others spiritually to serve

◎ What to Look Out For

Not valuing the gift, which is not always visible

Not remembering the gift is a *spiritual* gift, and thus might be seen only in the spiritual realm

Viewing prayer as a substitute for action

Having a judgmental attitude toward those not as dedicated to prayer

Knowledge

The ability to receive and share God's knowledge and insights for a specific situation and to communicate it effectively

◎ What It Looks Like

Knowing when a message is coming directly from God and not from themselves

Having supernatural insight into other people's situations

Being aware of words or images about a given situation before understanding them fully

Understanding or knowing things that couldn't be known with human abilities

◎ What to Look Out For

Feeling convinced of "knowing God's will"

Sharing a private message for someone where others can (and shouldn't) be hearing it

Feeling proud and forgetting that it's God's gift

Leadership

The ability to provide vision and direction for the body of Christ so that others see it and work together to make the vision happen

◎ What It Looks Like

Seeing and communicating the big picture

Seeing the end result before anything's been started

Sharing vision clearly and getting others involved quickly

Being the one assumed to be in charge, even when that's not officially the case

◎ What to Look Out For

Micromanaging

Ignoring the needs of those who help make the vision real

Not stepping back and listening to the Spirit before stepping forward

Not realizing that relationships are critical to success, and that they take time

Forgetting that the leader is the servant of all

Mercy

The divine empathy and compassion for those who suffer, and the ability to help those individuals both emotionally and practically

◎ What It Looks Like

Extending love and compassion to those who can't pay it back

Being drawn to the marginalized in society—the outcasts and outsiders

Sticking it out with people who have terminal illnesses or issues, and helping to relieve their suffering

Cheerfully serving those in difficult or unpleasant circumstances, without concern for recognition

◎ What to Look Out For

Becomingoverly protective of those in their care

Feeling unappreciated by those they help

Rejecting others who appear insensitive to the people they're caring for

Hating to say no, even when it's necessary

Rescuing people from difficulties that God might be using to teach them

Pastoring

The ability to give long-term care and guidance to people so they experience spiritual maturity and Christ-likeness

◎ **What It Looks Like**

Enjoying and gaining strength from being with, encouraging, and supporting others

Commiting to the long-term spiritual care and growth of others

Enjoying counseling and guiding others, with or without the benefit of a license

Leading by example, and walking others through it

◎ **What to Look Out For**

Being indecisive because of sensitivity to others

Inadvertently enabling others to become too dependent

"Protecting" others by making decisions for them

Struggling with letting go of others who are ready to move on

Having trouble turning people away, even when it cuts into time with family or friends or affects their own well-being

Prophecy

The divine ability to reveal and proclaim God's truth in a timely manner for others' understanding, correction, forewarning, or edification

◎ **What It Looks Like**

Being "prophetic," either by speaking about a future event or by speaking directly and insightfully about a current situation

Sharing critical messages from God that could lead to profound and immediate life change in others

Exhibiting authority in speaking God's truth, whether it's a biblical message or a word of knowledge

Exposing sin or deception in others for the purpose of reconciliation and resolution with God

◎ **What to Look Out For**

Pessimism and tendency to portray personal feelings as God's

Becoming prideful or self-centered with God, others, or both

Not remembering that his or her message may be rejected if it's not spoken with love and compassion

Not remembering that his or her message may be rejected even if it *is* spoken with love and compassion

Service

The ability to identify unmet practical needs in the church and beyond, using every available resource to do it

◎ What It Looks Like

Finding a way to meet other's practical needs

Being the "go-to" people when manpower (or woman-power) is needed to get things done

Loving the act of serving and seeing things get done

Willingness to rearrange personal schedules to make sure others get served

Seeing and addressing real needs before others even notice

◎ What to Look Out For

Neglecting their own needs in order to serve others

Inadvertently pushing other potential helpers to the side

Burning out because of inability to say no

Seeing people as projects rather than as people

Going around leadership to get things done

Teaching

The ability to understand, clearly explain, and help others apply the Word of God to their lives

◎ What It Looks Like

Communicating and applying biblical truth to every part of life

Effectively instructing, correcting, and equipping others

Communicating scriptural insights so others can see them clearly

Enjoying and feeling energized by extended times of study and reflection on God's Word

◎ What to Look Out For

Being a know-it-all and not allowing others to share insights

Communicating too much too soon

Promoting personal insights as biblical ones

Becoming focused on content to the point of overlooking the people they're trying to communicate it to

Forgetting that knowledge isn't the same as wisdom

Wisdom

The ability to apply spiritual truth promptly and effectively to specific situations

◎ What It Looks Like

Applying spiritual knowledge in specific and practical ways, and doing it promptly and incisively

Looking beyond the quick fix to future consequences of people's actions

Providing Christ-like solutions to spiritual and/or practical issues when they're needed most

◎ What to Look Out For

Becoming overly dependent on their own human wisdom rather than on God's wisdom

Imposing personal views upon others and calling them God's views

Not preventing others from becoming dependent on them rather than on God

Not being patient with others who lack wisdom

But What Does God Want Me to Do?

"*Take delight in the LORD, and he will give you your heart's desires*"
(PSALM 37:4).

In this session, we'll journey...

from ──────────────→ **to**

identifying the desires God has given us...

discovering how God might want to fulfill those desires in each of our lives.

Before gathering, make sure you have...

○ a variety of items that could be representative of personal interests of group members–at least enough for everyone ✳

○ newsprint tablet, blackboard, or white board

───────────────────────────

✳See **Leader Notes**, page 192.

Come and See

↓

(about 15 minutes)

Spread out all the items you've gathered before this session in the middle of your group, or somewhere nearby.

➤➤ **Welcome. Get into your groups. As you do, look over the items laid out before you. Grab one that represents something you enjoy doing. You don't have to spiritualize your choice—it's OK to enjoy something just because you enjoy it.**

Once you're in your groups, take about one minute each to share about the item you took, what it represents, and what it is you enjoy about that activity.

Allow three minutes for discussion, and then bring everyone back together. Ask for volunteers to share highlights and insights from their group discussion.

➤➤ **Last week we talked about the importance of letting God use us the way he wants to use us—the way he's built us. This session assumes you understand that session. And since we're going on that assumption, would someone please read Psalm 37:3-7?**

After your volunteer has read, say,

➤➤ **With that passage in mind, take a few seconds to read the quote on your group page. Then we'll discuss.**

Write everyone's answers to this last question on your white board. Then continue your discussion:

➤➤ **Hold those thoughts you've been sharing, because you'll need them later on. And for that matter, hold on to the item you took. You'll need that later, too.**

Last week you were alerted that this would be a work week. Well, it's time to get down to work. We've spent the last several weeks, both during our time together and in the time in between, exploring how God has built each of us—our gifts, our passions, our desires,

> *Likewise, it is my sense that many Christians are starting to suspect that they are stuck at the visitor's center. They suspect that they are traveling with Jesus but missing the adventure.*
>
> —Gary A. Haugen, Just Courage

and the things God wants to accomplish through us. This week we're going to take all the pieces God has given us and start figuring out how they fit together.

I hope you've all brought your forms because you'll need them. If not, work with what you remember, and focus on the others in your group, because you're going to help each other work through this together. Get back into your groups, and let's begin.

Love God, and do whatever you please.

—Augustine, "Sermon on 1 John 7, 8"

 Psalm 37:3-7

◎ What makes sense to you about both statements? What makes you feel uneasy about them?

◎ What helps us know whether our desires are really God's, too? Give examples.

◎ If our desires really *are* God's desires, what reasons would God have for *not* fulfilling them?

Seek and Find

(about 30 minutes)

》Look at the "Putting the Pieces Together" pages of your books. On the first page, fill in the four spiritual gifts that scored highest in the surveys you did on your own. Then enter the top three gifts that others say they see in you, based on the "I See You" pages they returned to you. Then compare your two lists. Where are others confirming what you're seeing? Or what are others consistently noticing that you hadn't noticed but are now starting to wonder about? Then look over both lists. Pick the top three gifts that are coming up, and enter them into the column on the right.

Then go to the next page. Think about the things we've shared over the last couple of weeks. What gets you excited? Who has God given you the biggest heart for? What can you imagine being able to do? Write your top three of those things, and rewrite your top three potential spiritual gifts next to them.

You'll have 10 minutes to do this part. If you have time left over, start thinking through the section at the bottom of Part II—what are some ways your gifts and your passions could come together for God's glory? It might be something you're already doing. It may be something you've thought about but haven't yet taken the next step to do. It may be something you've thought of just now. And you might think of something that seems totally off-the-wall at first— but don't throw it out just yet.

If you don't get to that final section yet, it's OK—you'll have time to work through it with your group later on. Everyone understand? (If not, make sure everyone does understand before moving on.)

OK, go! I'll let you know when 10 minutes are up.

After 10 minutes, say:

》Now take another 15 minutes in your groups to share what God has shown each of you. After each person shares, take a few minutes to come up with ideas for that final section together. How might God want to put those gifts together in him or her? Don't feel you have to come up with the perfect answer; just start throwing ideas out there. You never know what God might show you to help each other.

Make sure everyone gets the chance to share. I'll let you know when five, and then 10, minutes are up, to help you stay on track. So have at it, and good luck!

Let groups know when 5, and then 10 minutes have passed. After 15 minutes, gather everyone's attention, and ask groups to share some of the things they've discovered about God, themselves, and each other.

Putting the Pieces Together

PART I

The four spiritual gifts I most see in myself:

1. _____

2. _____

3. _____

4. _____

Based on what I see in myself, and what others see in me, I believe my top three spiritual gifts are:

1. _____

2. _____

3. _____

The three gifts others most see in me:

1. _____

2. _____

3. _____

Putting the Pieces Together

PART II

The three areas of my life or ministry that get me most excited are:

1. _____

2. _____

3. _____

My top three spiritual gifts (copy from previous page):

1. _____

2. _____

3. _____

Here are some ideas for how my gifts and passions might work together to serve God:

1. _____

2. _____

3. _____

4. _____

5. _____

Go

(about 20 minutes)

Ask for a volunteer to read 1 Corinthians 9:23–27, and then discuss these questions: ⟶

》Instead of our regular "Walk It Out" time, get back into your groups.

You've talked about some big things today. Some of you are ready to jump right into something new and exciting. Some of you might be feeling recharged after talking about things that matter to you and you're already involved with. Yet others of you might be thinking, All this is great, but I still don't have a clue what to do next. And that's OK, too.

The only wrong answer here is, "God doesn't care about where I'm at." So take time to share and to pray for one another's situations. Invite God into the process. After all, God is the one stirring all this up within you in the first place.

If it's appropriate to your situation, use the item you took at the beginning of this session as an offering to God. Hold it in front of you, and let God take that thing that brings pleasure or satisfaction to your life so it can bring God's pleasure to others' lives—and in the way God wants to.

Take your item home with you as a reminder that God wants to use every good thing in our lives to reveal his goodness to others.

When you're done praying, you're free to go [or hang out, if it's a small group]. **May God bless your time together and what he wants to do with each of you!**

✝ **1 Corinthians 9:23-27**

◎ Why is it important to have both desire and discipline when running a race of any kind? How do—or should—the two work together?

◎ Reflecting on everything you've shared today, which do you need more in your own race—desire or discipline? Or is it something else?

◎ What could most help you in training for your race right now?

Because God has given me these gifts and passions for a reason, I'll "Walk It Out" by:

_____

_____

_____

_____

_____

Go Deeper

To dig deeper into how to put together the gifts and passions God has given each of us, here are some great resources:

S.H.A.P.E.: Finding and Fulfilling Your Unique Purpose for Life by Erik Rees (Zondervan)

Experiencing God: Knowing and Doing the Will of God by Henry Blackaby, Richard Blackaby, and Claude King (B&H)

Network: The Right People, in the Right Places, for the Right Reasons, at the Right Time by Bruce L. Bugbee, Don Cousins, and Wendy Seidman (Zondervan)

Unleash Your Church! by Paul Ford (ChurchSmart)

Desiring God: Meditations of a Christian Hedonist by John Piper (Multnomah)

Without Love, I'm Nothing

If I had the gift of prophecy, and if I understood all of God's secret plans and possessed all knowledge, and if I had such faith that I could move mountains, but didn't love others, I would be nothing" (1 CORINTHIANS 13:2).

In this session, we'll journey...

from ⟶ **to**

revisiting the need for a servant heart in everything we do, inside the church or out...

understanding ways to let God's love for us flow out wherever we serve.

Before gathering, make sure you have...

○ 6 dominoes for each person✱

○ a table or other flat surface for every 2 to 3 of your groups. (The floor is OK, too.)

Optional activities (choose one or both):

○ **Option A:** Do "Go" as is (see page 124)

○ **Option B:** DVD of *How the Grinch Stole Christmas* (see page 129)

✱See **Leader Notes**, page 193.

Come and See

(about 15 minutes)

Have people get into their groups.

》 **Think about your last bad experience while going out to eat, whether it was at a four-star restaurant or a fast-food joint. And then discuss these questions together:**

Allow five minutes for discussion, and then come back to discuss highlights and insights from your discussion time.

》 **We all mess up from time to time, even when we're trying to serve others. And as we begin to take our gifts and passions and venture out into the unknown, it's pretty much guaranteed that we'll fail on occasion. But part of moving forward—maybe the biggest part—is how we respond to those failures, because it reveals a lot about what our motivations really are. If we're simply trying to fulfill a task, make ourselves look good, or save face, we'll usually end up looking more like those "servants" who gave us all such memorably bad experiences.**

So let's explore further. Would someone read 1 Corinthians 12:27 through 13:3?

》 **Let's look more at how the love of Jesus can spill over into every other part of our lives—and into each other's lives as well.**

Fall in love with a group of people who are marginalized and suffering, and then you won't have to worry about which cause you need to protest. Then the issues will choose you.

—Shane Claiborne, The Irresistible Revolution

Come and See

◎ First of all, what went wrong?

◎ What could have been prevented, and how? How could—or did—others help make things right, even if it wasn't their fault?

◎ Would you give that place another chance? Why or why not?

 1 Corinthians 12:27–13:3

◎ Think about a time *you* did all the right things for someone, but not in a loving way. What were the results?

◎ What would you do differently if you had another chance?

◎ Go back to verse 27, and reflect once more on your dining experience. Why is it important to help each other rather than leave others to fend for themselves? What are some of the challenges in doing that?

Seek and Find

(about 25 minutes)

Give each person six dominoes, and break into groups. Have existing groups team together, so there's at least four or five people in each group for this activity.

》 Use all your dominoes to set up a sequence in which they'll all fall once the first domino has tipped over (but don't tip it over yet!). Be creative— make it twist and turn however you like. Take a minute to set up your sequence.

After one minute, ask for a volunteer to read 1 John 4:7-12. Then have groups discuss these questions:

Give groups three minutes to discuss, and then gather every-one's attention, keeping them with their groups. Ask a couple volunteers to share their answers.

Let groups tip over their dominoes, and watch as their sequences are completed. Ask everyone to take a single domino, then have them take 10 minutes to read 1 John 3:16-20 and discuss these questions:

Come back together as a larger group, and share any highlights or questions from your subgroup discussion.

1 John 4:7-12

◎ Look at your setup. Which domino would you be—the starter, the last one to fall, or somewhere in between? Explain your choice.

◎ How is your sequence like or unlike being connected with other Christians?

◎ What's one way you've seen Jesus' love for you "topple over" into your love for others?

 1 John 3:16-20

◎ How does John's command to "give up our lives for our brothers and sisters" make you feel? Challenged? Frightened? Overwhelmed? Something else?

◎ Regardless of your reaction, why is it still important to do it?

◎ Think of someone you've had a particularly hard time showing Jesus' love to. What's one practical way you could "give up your life" for that person?

Go

(about 20 minutes)

If you've chosen to do **Option A**, *read on.*
If you're doing **Option B**, *go to page 129.*

》 Let's reflect once more on our last few sessions, and especially on those things you're passionate about that you've shared in your groups. What gets you excited? Who has God given you the biggest heart for? What can you imagine being able to do? Quietly, to yourselves, think about the one thing that's most important to you right now. (Pause for about 10 seconds.)

Now try to take yourself out of the equation for a minute as we discuss this question:

》 Let's circle back to Paul's description of what love in action looks like. We probably all know it: 1 Corinthians 13:4-13.

Read the passage to your group.

》 OK, go ahead and insert yourself back into your situation, as we discuss this question:

◎ If someone else were doing it, what would love in action look like in that situation or with that person or persons you're thinking about right now?

✝ **1 Corinthians 13:4-13**

◎ Realistically—not ideally—what would *your* love in action in that situation look like? What, if anything, needs to change?

◎ Who could help you bring more love into that situation or relationship, either by coming alongside you or by his or her example?

Walk It Out

(about 5 minutes)

》 The following options are here to help you put what you've learned into practice. But if God has prompted you to do something else through this session, then by all means do that!

GROUP ▼

choose 1:

□ know it

John's epistles speak of love in action. So spend time with that message this week. Read a chapter each day (or read all three "books" every day—seven short chapters). Reflect on what it means to love Jesus—and how the proof is in the way you love others. As the Spirit reveals areas for you to grow in, ask God's help in getting you there.

□ live it

Sit down sometime this week and write down every way you can think of that God shows his love to you. Maybe it's in a quiet moment with God; maybe it's through laughter with your close friends; maybe it's a special verse that speaks to your heart. As you discover new examples during the week, write them down, and stop and thank God each time. At week's end, read over everything you've written, and thank God some more. Share what you've discovered with someone else.

□ share it

Have you hurt someone? Is there hatred or resentment you need to be forgiven for—or forgive others for? Pray about this now, asking God to change your attitude toward that person. Commit to replacing hate or anger with God's love. Then invite that person over for dinner or out to a cup of coffee, and bring God's forgiveness into that relationship.

Form pairs, select the option you'd like to take on this week, and share your choice with your partner. Write what you plan to do in the space provided, and make plans to connect with your partner before the next session to check in and encourage each other. Take five minutes to do that now.

☐ **go for it** "Give up" your life for someone in a practical way this week. Find a way to show compassion to someone in need. Fill a gas tank, buy a hot meal, or just provide a listening ear. Commit to doing something meaningful that requires your intentional time and effort.

☐ **do it together**
Hold a social event as a group. Plan something fun, such as a cookout, Super Bowl party, game night, or holiday celebration. As a group, invite not-yet Christian (and Christian) friends, family members, *whomever* God has placed on your heart during this session. Make it a time to celebrate God's love and your love for each other (even those you're meeting for the first time!)

...or think of your own!

Because loving God means—and helps me in—loving others, I'll "Walk It Out" by:

_____

_____

_____

_____

_____

Walk It Out continued

Come back together as a group, and lead everyone in prayer.

prayer⊙

》 Lord, please help us all gain a deeper appreciation of your love for us. And as we understand your love more deeply, help us all know how to show the love of Jesus to those *we* care most about. Amen.

SEEING IT DIFFERENTLY

LEADER   Try "Go"-ing this way: Watch a scene from the movie *How the Grinch Stole Christmas* (the original cartoon version). Cue it to 20:04, as the narrator says, "And the Grinch put a hand to his ear..." Stop the clip at 24:14, as the Grinch serves the roast beast to Cindy Lou Who. Discuss these questions:

GROUP

◎ When has love given you the strength to do things you couldn't have otherwise done? Give examples.

◎ What would other people see if *your* heart "grew three times"?

Let's circle back to Paul's description of what love in action looks like in 1 Corinthians 13:4-13.

GROUP

✝ **1 Corinthians 13:4–13**

◎ What things grow—or break—*your* heart? Why?

◎ "Who" has God given you the biggest heart for? And "who" could help you bring even more love into that situation or relationship, either by coming alongside you or by his or her example?

Go on to "Walk It Out." It starts on page 126.

Go Deeper

To dig deeper into how you can put your love into action, here are some great resources:

Outflow: Outward-Focused Living in a Self-Focused World by Steve Sjogren and Dave Ping (Group)

Crazy Love: Overwhelmed by a Relentless God by Francis Chan (Cook)

They Will Know Us by Our Love: Service Ideas for Small Groups (Group)

Surrender to Love: Discovering the Heart of Christian Spirituality by David G. Benner (InterVarsity)

Sharing the Gift

" *I am fully convinced, my dear brothers and sisters, that you are full of goodness. You know these things so well you can teach each other all about them"* (ROMANS 15:14).

In this session, we'll journey...

from ──────────→ **to**

understanding the importance
of giving (and receiving)
encouragement...

identifying practical steps to both
give *and* receive encouragement
from others.

Before gathering, make sure you have...

○ a snack that (eventually) everyone will enjoy✳

○ newsprint tablet, blackboard, or white board

──────────────

✳See **Leader Notes**, page 194, for details.

Come and See

(about 10 minutes)

》 Welcome back. We've already done a lot of investigating into how God has built each of us. We've also looked at how important love is as we put those gifts into action—so that we not only do what God has created us to do but we also do those things in such a way that our hearts truly reflect God's heart. So today let's take the next step.

》 We all have something to offer one another. God has created each of us uniquely, so we can fit together perfectly to accomplish whatever God wants to accomplish through us. And yet, it usually takes some effort to discover what each person's real contributions are, or can be. It would be great if we all instantly liked and understood each other, but the fact is, it takes time.

The good news is *it's worth your time*. So let's reflect on why it's so important to be connected to each other, especially as Christians, and how we can encourage each other and help make those connections happen.

> *We preach teamwork, but we idolize individualism.*
>
> —Jean Lipman-Blumen, Connective Leadership

Come and See

◎ When have *you* felt left out? Choose any kind of situation you like. What could you have offered that you felt wasn't being asked for or wanted?

◎ On the other hand, when have you kept your gifts or abilities to yourself—like I just hoarded our snack? What could you have offered that really *was* needed, and why didn't you?

Seek and Find

(about 30 minutes)

» **Get into your groups. Read the following list of passages, and then discuss the questions that follow. Let's take 15 minutes for that and then come back together.** ───────────────

- Romans 15:13-14
- 1 Corinthians 12:14-26
- 1 Thessalonians 5:11-22
- Hebrews 10:24-25
- 1 Peter 4:7-11

After 15 minutes, come back together. Ask for groups' answers to the question, "What should that encouragement look like?" Write down everyone's responses. If you have time, ask groups to share other highlights and insights from their discussion time.

> *In some sense the most benevolent, generous person in the world seeks his own happiness in doing good to others, because he places his happiness in their good... Thus when they are happy, he feels it; he partakes with them, and is happy in their happiness.*
>
> —Jonathan Edwards

» **You've just discussed the importance—and the joy—of working together and bringing all our different gifts to the table.**

So let's discuss another question: ───────────────

Write everyone's responses to *this* question, too. ───────────────

Romans 15:13–14; 1 Corinthians 12:14–26; 1 Thessalonians 5:11–22; Hebrews 10:24–25; 1 Peter 4:7–11

◎ What images of encouragement do you see in these passages?

◎ What should that encouragement look like? Give both biblical and personal examples.

◎ How are the things we described different when God is involved, rather than when it's just us?

◎ When have you seen people join together for a bigger purpose? How did the things we wrote down come into play?

◎ What keeps these moments from happening more often in our lives?

◎ What do you think of Paul's statement in Romans 15:14, that your "brothers and sisters...are full of goodness"? How would (or does) believing it change the way you approach and work together with them?

Seek and Find continued

>> We need each other. There's no way around it. God built us not only to serve him, but to serve him together. Encouragement—openly recognizing that God built the person next to you the way *he* wanted, and for *his* good purposes—is a lot of the glue that holds us together as we serve. You've spent the last several weeks together in groups that were created to help you accomplish just that. So let's take full advantage of that right now.

It is the fellowship of the Cross to experience the burden of the other. If one does not experience it, the fellowship he belongs to is not Christian. If any member refuses to bear that burden, he denies the law of Christ.

—Dietrich Bonhoeffer, Life Together

Go

(about 20 minutes)

Ask for a volunteer to read Ephesians 4:7–16, and then ask people to get back into their groups.

》 You've been together several weeks now—and possibly have known each other far longer than that. Either way, you've probably begun to discover some new things about each other. We're going to take a few minutes to recognize that.

Figure out whose first name comes first in the alphabet. The rest of the group: Share the positive things you see in that person. If you see a spiritual gift, tell that person what you're seeing and how you've seen him or her live it out. If you're not that familiar with each other yet, pick a positive attribute you've already seen in that person, such as honesty, strength, humility, or even a particular talent or ability. No matter what it is, don't be shy today in letting that person know what a special gift he or she really is.

Take 10 minutes to share with each other, and then let's come back together.

After 10 minutes, gather everyone's attention, keeping everyone in their groups. Invite people to share highlights and insights from their discussion time. When you're done, have groups "Walk It Out" together.

Walk It Out

(about 5 minutes)

》 **The following options are here to help you put what you've learned into practice. But if God has prompted you to do something else through this session, then by all means do that!**

choose 1:

☐ know it

Spend some more time with this week's Bible passages. Meditate on them. Pray about them. How do they impact you? Will it mean getting out of your shell and putting yourself out there? Or does it mean letting go of control so others can bring their unique gifts alongside to help you? Does it mean something else? Spend time using God's Word as a catalyst to finding (and pursuing) the answers God is offering you.

☐ live it

Find ways to support others in your church or group who are in need—as you would a member of your own family. Take a pot of soup to someone who's sick. Make a phone call to encourage someone who's hurting. Take a couple of bags of groceries or a gift card to someone who's struggling financially. Or...what unique way might God be showing you?

☐ share it

Is there a friend or co-worker facing a difficult choice or circumstance? Commit to praying for that person specifically about those choices, and let him or her *know* that you're praying. If it's appropriate, put that person in touch with members of your group or church who have the gifts and talents to help. It would build both sides up and probably be a pleasant surprise for both, too.

Form pairs, select the option you'd like to take on this week, and share your choice with your partner. Write what you plan to do in the space provided, and make plans to connect with your partner before the next session to check in and encourage each other. Take five minutes to do that now.

☐ **go for it** Think about how you could stretch your boundaries this week. Could you help fill a leadership role in church or elsewhere? Could you get involved in service project? Is there a ministry in your church where you could give someone a much-needed break this week? Commit to discovering how you could join with others to support the gifts they're already exercising—even if they *don't* yet know Jesus. And commit to taking that step.

☐ **do it together**
Become an ally of an organization or cause in town that really needs support. It doesn't have to be a Christian organization—in fact, it may prove to be more powerful if it isn't. How can you support your police or fire departments or an organization that specializes in showing mercy and compassion to the more marginalized members of your community? Be creative, and then be involved.

...or think of your own!

Because I'm here to both encourage others and to be encouraged, I'll "Walk It Out" by:

_____

_____

_____

_____

Walk It Out continued

Come back together as a group. Pass your snack around a second time, and have everyone receive a sample, whether they eat it or not. As they hold their snacks, reread Ephesians 4:14-16.

prayer⊙

Then lead your group in prayer, thanking God that "he makes the whole body fit together perfectly." Ask God to help each person see new ways he or she can help other Christians "so that the whole body is healthy and growing and full of love." Ask God to open everyone's eyes to opportunities to build up others who don't know Jesus and to use all of you to show those people how Jesus wants to build *them,* too.

To dig deeper into how God wants us all to encourage one another, here are some great resources:

Encouraging Others: Biblical Models for Caring by Lin Johnson (Random House)

Group's BibleSense™: Ephesians: Seeing Ourselves in Jesus (Group)

The Joy of Encouragement: Unlock the Power of Building Others Up by David Jeremiah (Multnomah)

Emotionally Healthy Spirituality: Unleash the Power of Authentic Life in Christ by Peter Scazzero (Thomas Nelson)

Fill 'Er Up!

Yes, I am the vine; you are the branches. Those who remain in me, and I in them, will produce much fruit. For apart from me you can do nothing" (JOHN 15:5).

In this session, we'll journey...

from —————————————→ **to**
recognizing the need to "keep your tank filled" as you move forward in Jesus...

determining how we can each best stay connected to God.

Before gathering, make sure you have...

○ enough ready-made cookie dough for everyone to have more than one cookie✱

○ newsprint tablet, blackboard, or white board

✱See **Leader Notes**, page 195, for details.

Come and See

(about 10 minutes)

Invite people to take one snack each (or more, if you have enough), even if they don't intend to eat it. Then ask them to get into their groups and discuss these questions: ——————

Allow five minutes, and then come back together to share highlights and insights from your discussion time.

> *God's insistence that we ask Him to give us help so that He gets glory (Psalm 50:15) forces on us the startling fact that we must beware of serving God and take special care to let Him serve us, lest we rob Him of His glory.*
>
> *—John Piper,*
> *Desiring God*

》 Whether you're in a good place or a bad one right now, it's always important to remember that no matter how hard we try—no matter how important our ministry is to others or how important it makes us feel to be doing it—we won't get far without God's power. Or without recognizing that everything we do should glorify God.

***Everything* we do—no matter how mundane or normal it might seem to us—can be an act of worship. Everything we *truly* do for God is worship. But we need to stay connected to God to do it. And as incredible as it sounds, we need to allow God to serve *us*—to give us the things we need so that we're *really serving him* back.**

As we reconnect and stay connected with God, the Spirit gives us the power and direction we need to do the things God has built us for. Without that power, it's just us thinking we're doing God a favor. So let's refuel and move forward together.

◎ Which cookies (or dough) did you choose? Why?

◎ How would you describe your *spiritual* state right now? Baked to a golden brown and ready to serve? Half-baked? Burnt to a crisp? Explain your answer.

Seek and Find

(about 30 minutes)

» **But first, let's discuss a couple more things.**

Write everyone's answers on your white board. Keep all the answers to one side of your board—you'll need the other side later on.

Then ask:

Write any additional answers beneath the answers to your first question.

> *Without depending on God we can do nothing, not even can we live as Christians for a single day.*
>
> *—Watchman Nee, The Messenger of the Cross*

» **Now let's begin to refuel by spending time in God's Word together. Get back into your groups. Read the following passages, and then discuss the questions that follow. Let's take 15 minutes for that.**

• Psalm 50:7-15

• Isaiah 40:21-31

• John 15:1-8

• 2 Corinthians 12:6-10

• Revelation 2:1-5

After 15 minutes, come back together to share highlights and insights from your discussion time.

◎ What things just seem to drain all the energy out of you whenever they happen?

◎ Which of the situations we've listed tend to pull you away from God rather than cause you to lean on him? (Be more specific than "all of them.") Are there any situations we haven't mentioned yet?

 Psalm 50:7-15; Isaiah 40:21-31; John 15:1-8; 2 Corinthians 12:6-10; Revelation 2:1-5

◎ Which of these passages resonates most with you right now? Why do you think that is?

◎ We've already talked about circumstances that pull us away from God. When have difficult circumstances pushed you *closer* to God? Talk about it.

◎ Why do you think your reactions during those times were so different from the times you pulled away from God?

◎ How can you respond differently to the things that do tend to pull you away from God?

Go

(about 20 minutes)

Ask for a volunteer to read Philippians 4:1-13. Then discuss:——

Write everyone's answers on the other side of your board or pad, acknowledging each person's contribution as you do so.

Philippians 4:1-13

◎ What ways does Paul encourage us to connect with God in this passage?

◎ How have you experienced God's peace in the past by doing these things?

◎ Which of these things do you have a hard time "putting into practice"? How would doing them help you draw from God's strength, no matter what you're dealing with right now?

Walk It Out

(about 5 minutes)

» **The following options are here to help you put what you've learned into practice. But if God has prompted you to do something else through this session, then by all means do that!**

choose 1:

☐ know it

Spend some more time in this week's readings, especially those that are speaking to you the loudest right now. What is God trying to tell you, and what are you going to do about it? Spend time reconnecting with God and finding out the answer to that question this week. Then take the steps to make God's direction your reality.

☐ live it *and* share it

Think again about how you normally connect with God and what other ways you might do so. Then try this: Spend an entire day worshipping God in those new ways. At some point during the day, share with someone else what you're doing and why. Letting others know you're making God—and only God—your priority might help them do the same.

☐ go for it

How can you connect with God—*in public*? This idea isn't for everyone, but if you're musically gifted or don't mind praying with others looking on, find a nearby park, and invite a group (maybe *this* one!) to sing, pray, or worship along with you. Be respectful of others' personal space, but don't be afraid to let your faith and joy come out. Sure, some passers-by could be put off, but others might be curious about what (or Who) makes you tick. Who knows? You might even get some additional participants—or at least the opportunity to share the Source of your joy.

Form pairs, select the option you'd like to take on this week, and share your choice with your partner. Write what you plan to do in the space provided, and make plans to connect with your partner before the next session to check in and encourage each other. Take five minutes to do that now.

☐ **do it together** Plan a weekend (or at least an all-day) retreat with your group. It doesn't have to be on a secluded mountainside, but it should be somewhere far enough away that people feel they're escaping distractions. Be sure to set aside not only group times for eating, recreation, prayer, and worship, but also at least one extended time (an hour or more) for people to get alone with God to receive his guidance, meditate upon the Word, and appreciate creation. Be sure to gather after this solitary time to share what God may be saying to each of you.

...or think of your own!

Because I need to stay connected to God, I'll "Walk It Out" by:

_____

_____

_____

_____

_____

_____

_____

Walk It Out continued

prayer⊙   Come back together as a group. Reread John 15:5, then take some time to confess as a group when you've let "doing"—even "doing for God"—disconnect you from Jesus' strength. Ask for God's forgiveness and guidance to help you stay connected, even when other things in life try to pull you away.

Go Deeper

To dig deeper into how to stay refueled daily in Jesus, here are some great resources:

Growing Out: From Disciples to Disciplers; Season 1: Growing in Jesus by Carl Simmons (Group)

Deep-Rooted in Christ: The Way of Transformation by Joshua Choonmin Kang (InterVarsity)

Sacred Pathways by Gary L. Thomas (Zondervan)

The Good and Beautiful God: Falling in Love With the God Jesus Knows by James Bryan Smith (InterVarsity)

The Practice of the Presence of God by Brother Lawrence (Xulon)

A Question of Balance

So don't worry about these things, saying, 'What will we eat? What will we drink? What will we wear?' These things dominate the thoughts of unbelievers, but your heavenly Father already knows all your needs. Seek the Kingdom of God above all else, and live righteously, and he will give you everything you need. So don't worry about tomorrow, for tomorrow will bring its own worries. Today's trouble is enough for today" (MATTHEW 6:31-34).

In this session, we'll journey...

from ————————————→ **to**
understanding the importance   identifying areas where we can
of balancing and managing our   start doing it.
time...

Before gathering, make sure you have...

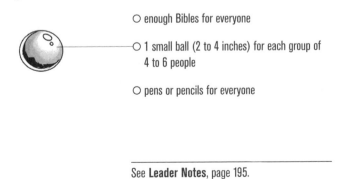

O enough Bibles for everyone

O 1 small ball (2 to 4 inches) for each group of
   4 to 6 people

O pens or pencils for everyone

See **Leader Notes**, page 195.

Come and See

(about 10 minutes)

>> **Get into your groups. Then find another group, and get together to form a larger group with them.**

Give groups time to gather. If you have an uneven number of groups, try to get three of your smaller groups to gather together.

>> **Now each of you take your Bible in both hands and hold it out front of you. With both hands.**

Give a Bible to anyone who doesn't have one. Once everyone is holding a Bible, give a ball to one member of each group. Don't give any instructions as to whether people should let go of their Bibles or not.

>> **Now pass your ball to the next person, and keep passing it around your entire group. When you're done, take 10 minutes to discuss these questions:**

Bring everyone back together after 10 minutes, and share highlights and insights from your discussion time.

>> **Sometimes being overloaded is unavoidable—we have deadlines; there's a family crisis; sometimes everything in our lives comes to a head all at once. But many times we're overloaded as a result of our own choices. We take on as much as we think we can handle, but it turns out we thought wrong. Or we really did take on as much as we could handle—but the unexpected hit, and we didn't have the physical, mental, or emotional resources left to deal with anything more.**

We experienced no difficulty at all in losing sight of what God wants us to do! Just a little overwork—indeed we might say, just a little extra work for God—is all too capable of diverting our eyes from that ultimate vision.

—Watchman Nee,
Changed Into His
Likeness

◎ How did you "grab" the ball when it came to you? Why did you do it that way instead of some other way?

◎ What do you normally do when you have too much to handle—let go of one thing to do another, or try to somehow do everything?

◎ Likewise, spiritually, how do you deal with having too much on your plate—let go of your time with God, let other responsibilities drop, or somehow try to do it all? How well does that work for you?

Last week we focused on our need to stay fueled spiritually. That's our first priority, and learning to rely on Jesus goes a long way toward getting us through whatever challenges we face. But God also wants us to use wisdom in choosing our priorities and in deciding how much we really can handle, so our lives don't get overloaded and imbalanced in the first place.

Let's take a closer look at the choices we make and why we make them. Then let's see what adjustments God may be asking each of us to make.

Seek and Find

(about 25 minutes)

Discuss: ────────────────────────────→

》 Let's put our Bibles to a better use now. We're going to read the following passages together. After each passage, we'll stop to briefly discuss these three questions:

• **What's the problem here?**

• **At what point does it *become* a problem?**

• **What's God's answer to the problem?**

Ask for volunteers to read the following passages: Deuteronomy 8:10-18; Matthew 6:24-34; Matthew 11:28-30; Luke 10:38-42; and James 1:2-8. After reading each passage, stop and discuss the questions above. ────────→

》 Now that we've looked at these passages together, let's talk through a few more questions: ────────→

◎ Think about a time you felt stretched past the breaking point. Looking back at it now, how did you get to that point? How did you get past it? What could you have done differently?

For each passage, answer the following:

◎ What's the problem here?

◎ At what point does it *become* a problem?

◎ What's God's answer to the problem?

....

 Deuteronomy 8:10-18

 Matthew 6:24-34

 Matthew 11:28-30

 Luke 10:38-42

 James 1:2-8

◎ Which of these passages hits closest to where you're at right now? Why?

◎ Based on what we've just discussed, what should your response be—and what would that look like for you specifically?

Go

(about 25 minutes)

Make sure everyone has a pen or pencil.

» **We've talked about the things that stretch us and throw us out of balance and what God has to say about each of those circumstances. Now let's discuss what we might be able to do about the things we're dealing with. We're going to start by doing a little dreaming.**

On page 157, you'll see an empty pie chart. You're going to fill in what you'd *like* **your typical day to look like, if it were up to you. Be realistic—don't put in 12 hours of sleep followed by 12 hours of rest. But dream a little, too. What good things do you wish you could give more time toward but just don't seem to right now?**

There's a list of general ideas in the margin to help you think this through. Use as many of them as you want or add your own. Be as specific as you'd like. Let's take three minutes to do this, on your own.

Give people three minutes to work on the first chart, and then gather their attention. Ask:

» **OK, let's do this again. Only this time, you're going to make your chart represent how your life is** *really* **going. Take another two minutes to do that right now.**

Allow another two minutes, and then ask people to get into their groups.

Where *Does* the Time Go?

*(and where would you **like** it to go?)*

- work (including commute)
- sleep
- ministry or service
- eating (including prep time)
- TV, Internet, texting, or gaming
- Bible study and prayer
- family time (where the family actually *gets* your attention)
- "alone time" with your spouse
- exercise
- chores
- what else?

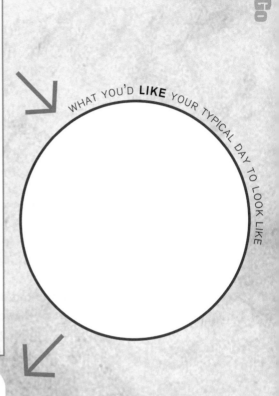

WHAT YOU'D **LIKE** YOUR TYPICAL DAY TO LOOK LIKE

◎ Based on the chart you just drew, what things matter most to you?

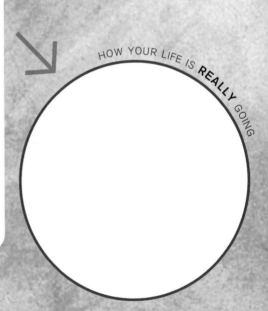

HOW YOUR LIFE IS **REALLY** GOING

Go continued

» Instead of our usual "Walk It Out" time, you're going to spend some time wrestling together with what you've just learned—or are about to learn—about yourselves. Discuss the questions on your group page, and then take the time to pray for one another about the gaps between where you want to be and where you are right now. Pray that God would reveal what things you can let go of, as well as multiply the time you have so you can serve God and others you care about in the way God is calling you to—without damaging yourself in the process.

When you're done discussing and praying, you're free to quietly leave or quietly hang out until everyone's finished.

◎ What's the biggest difference between the second chart and the first one?

◎ What do you think would be different if your life were more like your first chart? How would *you* be different?

◎ Be honest: What's *really* stopping you from making these changes? What do you think is your first step toward addressing those issues or attitudes?

Because God can use a balanced life more easily than an imbalanced one, I'll "Walk It Out" by:

_____

_____

_____

_____

_____

_____

_____

To dig deeper into how to bring (and keep) balance in your lives, here are some great resources:

Boundaries: When to Say Yes, How to Say No, to Take Control of Your Life by Henry Cloud and John Townsend (Zondervan)

Freedom From Tyranny of the Urgent by Charles E. Hummel (InterVarsity)

Margin: Restoring Emotional, Physical, Financial, and Time Reserves to Overloaded Lives by Richard Swenson (NavPress)

Freedom of Simplicity: Finding Harmony in a Complex World by Richard Foster (HarperOne)

The Importance of Being You

You must warn each other every day, while it is still 'today,' so that none of you will be deceived by sin and hardened against God" (HEBREWS 3:13).

In this session, we'll journey...

from ⟶ **to**

examining the importance
(and uniqueness) of spiritual
friendships...

deepening our relationships with
the Christians we need and the
Christians who need us.

Before gathering, make sure you have...

Optional activities (in both cases, choose one or both):

Come and See

○ **Option A:** Opening activity and discussion (see page 162)

○ **Option B:** DVD of *It's a Wonderful Life* (see page 171)

Go

○ **Option A:** Do Go as is (see page 166)

○ **Option B:** Another scene from *It's a Wonderful Life* (see page 172)

See **Leader Notes**, page 195.

Come and See

(about 20 minutes)

If you've chosen to do **Option A**, *read on.*
If you're doing **Option B**, *go to page 171.*

Have people get into their groups.

> *When life on earth is ending, people don't surround themselves with objects. What we want around us is people—people we love and have relationships with. In our final moments we all realize that relationships are what life is all about. Wisdom is learning that truth sooner rather than later.*
>
> —Rick Warren,
> The Purpose-
> Driven Life

》 **I'd like everyone to close their eyes.** (Pause.)

Now I want you to think about a time you went through a crisis or an emergency. For some of you, that might be right now. Some of you may need to reach back further, but get that situation in your heads. Remember the details of it, the emotions you experienced, the conflicting thoughts you had—or maybe just the same thought you had over and over. (Pause for 30 seconds.)

Let's bring that situation into the present (for those of us not already there). Think about this question: Who would you call right now, if you were going through that situation? (Pause another 15 seconds.)

OK, you can open your eyes. In your groups, discuss these questions. Don't go on to the second question until you're finished discussing the first one.

After 10 minutes, come back together, and share highlights and insights from your discussion time.

》 **This session might well be the most important one you'll study in this entire season. No matter how gifted we might be, no matter how strong we think we are (or how strong we think we have to be), we all hit places in our lives where we can't do it alone.**

◎ Who did you think of to call, and why?

◎ If you didn't mention someone in this group, why didn't you?

And the fact of the matter is, God never *intended* us to do it alone. God created us to develop friendships with those we can trust, where everything's on the table, and together we can bring those things to God.

If you already have friendships like that, you know how precious and rare they truly are. As we develop real spiritual friendships—as we walk alongside other true disciples of Jesus—God turns us into disciplers.

Let's discover together what those relationships look like and how we can aim at developing them, together.

Seek and Find

(about 20 minutes)

Discuss this question: ───────────────────────

Read the following passages together, and discuss these
questions: ──────────────────────────────────────

- Proverbs 27:5-6, 9-10, 17   - James 5:16
- 1 Corinthians 16:13-18   - 1 John 1:6-7
- Hebrews 3:12-14

> To believe you can
> make disciples or
> develop true maturity
> in others without some
> form of accountability
> is like believing that
> you can raise children
> without discipline, run
> a company without
> rules, or lead an army
> without authority.
> Accountability is to
> the Great Commission
> what tracks are to a
> train.
>
> —Bill Hull,
> The Disciple
> Making Pastor

» **Get back into your groups, and take 10 minutes to
discuss the next question together. As you discuss,
don't just share your answers—help each other think
through other possible answers to this question:** ───────

After 10 minutes, bring everyone back together, and proceed to
"Go."

◎ What's the toughest thing about being a real friend to someone?

 Proverbs 27:5-6, 9-10, 17; 1 Corinthians 16:13-18; Hebrews 3:12-14; James 5:16; 1 John 1:6-7

◎ What differences do you see between how the Bible defines friendship and how we often define it?

◎ Where does God's definition of friendship look like ours? How can what we're already doing help us bring God deeper into the friendships we already have?

◎ Think of a relationship where you wish God played a bigger role, even (or especially) if you're already close to that person. What ideas from the Bible or from our discussion could help you invite God deeper into that relationship?

Go

(about 20 minutes)

If you've chosen to do **Option A**, *read on.*
If you're doing **Option B**, *go to page 172.*

>> We've looked at spiritual friendships from a more personal perspective so far today, because that's where most of us are. But we shouldn't stop there. Let's close—and prepare ourselves for our final session next week—with an example of how spiritual friendship could operate on a larger scale. And let's dream a little about what God might want to do. Can I have a volunteer to read Acts 2:44-47? ———

Acts 2:44-47

◎ What are some things we can accomplish as a larger group of friends, brothers, and sisters in Jesus that we can't do with only one or two other friends?

◎ If you knew you had the support, what things that you know you can't do on your own would you attempt—or help someone else attempt—for Jesus?

◎ Be honest: What stands in the way of your trying? And what's your first step toward doing something about it?

Walk It Out

(about 5 minutes)

》 **The following options are here to help you put what you've learned into practice. But if God has prompted you to do something else through this session, then by all means do that!**

choose 1:

☐ know it

Spend more time in today's Bible passages. Also take some time to reflect on the friendships you have right now, whether those friendships are with Christians or non-Christians. (We sometimes have trouble talking about God even with other Christians, you know.) What can you do to bring God more front-and-center in those relationships? Spend time asking God to show you where he's already at work in your relationships and how you can join in.

☐ live it

We'll make this one simple: You just went through this session. You know exactly whom you need to take your friendship to the next level with spiritually. Pray for the right words to open both of you up to that possibility, and then do it!

☐ share it

Sometimes being a friend means saying something that needs to be said. Look for an opportunity to speak the truth in love to someone (Ephesians 4:15). Be assertive (not aggressive) with someone who needs to hear a truth that may be difficult to share (and for that person to hear).

Form pairs, select the option you'd like to take on this week, and share your choice with your partner. Write what you plan to do in the space provided, and make plans to connect with your partner before the next session to check in and encourage each other. Take five minutes to do that now.

☐ ## go for it *and* do it together

We'll make this one simple, too: As you had the discussion during "Go," what dreams or hopes did you share (or at least think of)? What can you do to make it a reality, and who's willing to work alongside you (or at least support you in prayer) as you do that? Or who shared something that *you* could come alongside of? Get started right now.

...or think of your own!

Because God created us to have spiritual friendships, I'll "Walk It Out" by:

_____

_____

_____

_____

_____

_____

_____

Walk It Out continued

prayer⊙

Come back together as a group. Thank God for the friends he's given you both inside and outside the group, and ask for God's help in seeing how you can put Jesus at the center of each of those relationships.

Go Deeper

To dig deeper into how to develop spiritual friendships, here are some great resources:

Everybody's Normal Till You Get to Know Them by John Ortberg (Zondervan)

Discipleship Essentials: A Guide to Building Your Life in Christ by Greg Ogden (InterVarsity)

Search & Rescue: Becoming a Disciple Who Makes a Difference by Neil Cole (Baker)

Sacred Companions: The Gift of Spiritual Friendship & Direction by David G. Benner (InterVarsity)

Life Together by Dietrich Bonhoeffer (HarperSanFrancisco)

SEEING IT DIFFERENTLY
Come and See–Option B

LEADER   Instead of the opening activity and discussion in Come and See, watch a scene from the movie *It's a Wonderful Life.* Cue the movie to 1:32:11 (DVD Chapter 20), where George Bailey says, "I'm in trouble, Mr. Potter. I need help." Stop the clip at 1:35:11, when Potter's on the phone saying, "Bill? This is Potter."

GROUP

◎ If you were in an emergency situation, who would you call on, and why?

◎ Who thought of someone in this group? Why did or didn't you?

Pick up at the leader statement that begins, **This session might well be the most important...** It's on page 162.

SEEING IT DIFFERENTLY

Go–Option B

LEADER   Instead of doing Go as is, watch another scene from *It's a Wonderful Life*. Forward the movie to 2:04:50 (DVD Chapter 27), when Mary says, "Come on, George, come on downstairs."

Before playing the clip, say:

We've looked at spiritual friendships mostly from a one-on-one or smaller-group perspective so far today. But we shouldn't stop there. Let's close—and prepare ourselves for next week—with an example of how spiritual friendship could operate on a larger scale. Let's dream a little about what God might want to do.

Stop the clip at 2:08:51, when George says, "That's a Christmas present from a very dear friend of mine." Read Acts 2:44-47 and then discuss:

GROUP

 Acts 2:44-47

◉ What are some things we can accomplish as a larger group of friends, brothers, and sisters in Jesus that we can't do with only one or two other friends?

◉ If you knew you had the support, what things that you know you can't do on your own would you attempt—or help someone else attempt—for Jesus?

◉ Be honest: What stands in the way of your trying? And what's your first step toward doing something about it?

Have people go to Walk It Out. It starts on page 168.

Where Do We Go From Here?

They brought in the two disciples and demanded, 'By what power, or in whose name, have you done this?' " (ACTS 4:7).

In this session, we'll journey...

from ⟶ **to**
looking back at where God has
taken each of you over this past
season...

looking forward to where God
wants to take you from here.

Before gathering, make sure you have...

○ snacks that feature two or more things that go well
together.

Optional activities (choose one or both):

○ **Option A:** Do Go as is

 ○ **Option B:** DVD of *The Lord of the Rings: The Two
Towers* (see page 183)

See **Leader Notes**, page 196.

Come and See

(about 15 minutes)

Encourage people to sit with their groups as you begin this session.

》 Congratulations! You've made it through this part of the journey together! You've been together with the people in your groups for a couple of months now, and God has shown us a lot these past few months. So before we go any further, take a minute to congratulate one another, and let them know how much you've appreciated your time together with them.

Allow a minute for groups to celebrate and share.

》 Now let's talk about where God has taken us over the last few months and how he got us there. First take one more long look at the people in your groups. (Pause.) ————————————————

Keep people with their groups as you go to "Seek and Find."

Indeed, there comes a time in the life of every believer and of every church where a voice inside us simply asks, Now what?...*This is the supernatural moment when the rescued enter into their divine destiny as rescuers.*

—Gary A. Haugen,
Just Courage

◎ Looking back at it now, why do you think God put you with the others in your group?

◎ What things did you discover about each other that you probably wouldn't have known if you hadn't been working together?

◎ We've explored gifts, talents, passions—the hands and hearts God has given to us. How have you seen them modeled by the others in your groups?

Seek and Find

(about 30 minutes)

>> **We just took a step back to reflect on where God has taken each of us and on the people God gave us to walk alongside us. Let's take one more giant step back, together, and remember how we really got to this point and what we'll need to go any further.**

Last week we closed with a picture of the early church—one which often seems more like a dream than a reality. This week, let's look at a different snapshot of a very similar scene—one that might give us a better idea of how God could actually use us to achieve change in the world around us, no matter how impossible that looks to us right now.

Ask for one or more volunteers to read Acts 4:7–14, 23–37.

>> **Now close your eyes.** (Pause.) **For just a moment, put yourself in this scene. Don't worry about hostile religious leaders or the fact that you're not Peter. Let's not forget that Peter wasn't always the person we find in this passage either.**

Whatever's stopping you from putting yourself in this scene, block it out of your head. We've spent an entire season focusing on the gifts, the passions, and the heart God has given each of you, so let's have a little fun envisioning this. Where would you be in this scene? How could God have changed you from an observer to a participant here? (Pause for a few more moments.)

OK, let's talk about what God created in this scene and about what God wants to create with each of us.

Acts 4:7-14, 23-37

◎ Sticking to what's actually in God's Word here, what gifts and passions did you see play out during this scene? Name as many things as you can.

◎ Now let's shift back to our reflection time. How did you see God using the gifts and passions he's given *you* in this scene?

◎ Look again at verse 7, then at verses 10 to 12. How does Peter's reply answer your own doubts about being able to do what God might want you to do?

Seek and Find continued

Do not forget that the value and interest of life is not so much to do conspicuous things...as to do ordinary things with the perception of their enormous value.

—Pierre Teilhard de Chardin

» Now in your groups, reflect together on what God has shown you over this past season and why he's shown it to you. This will be your "Walk It Out" this week—and hopefully well beyond.

Look at the worksheet on your group page, called "Where Now, God?" You're going to spend time together with that now, first on your own and then with your groups. Don't approach this as if you need to have it all worked out. God doesn't expect that— and besides, even if you *think* you've got it worked out, God knows his plans better than you do. Simply capture as best you can where you sense God is leading you right now and what you think the next steps could look like.

You'll probably have way more to talk about than we can cover today, and that's OK. Set aside some time to get together and talk things through after this session, too. And take some more time to celebrate together what God has done through each of you. But today, let's start things moving.

Take 25 minutes to fill in the pages as best you can, and when you're ready, discuss what you wrote with your group. Be sure to share your answers to at least these two questions:

• Where do I think God is leading me next?

• What do I need most right now in order to get there?

Have at it, and may God bless your time together.

After 25 minutes, call everyone back together, and then move on to Go.

Where Now, God?

Looking Back

Refer to your worksheets in Session 7 for this section. Feel free to update, based on what God has shown you the past several weeks.

Here are some ideas for how my gifts and passions might work together to serve God:

1. _____

2. _____

3. _____

4. _____

5. _____

Looking at Where I Am

This is the most important thing God has shown me through the study:

_____

_____

_____

_____

Because of what God has shown me, this is the next step I see God leading me to take:

_____

_____

_____

_____

continued ▶

(continued from page 179)

Looking Ahead

Answer the following questions as honestly as you can, and be ready to be transparent with your group members about these issues as well. Bring it all out into God's light together.

Reality Check: Faith version

◎Am I willing to prayerfully wait for God to lead me into the next steps, rather than run ahead on my own strength? (Even if all my answers above were "I don't know"?) If not, what's holding me back?

◎Do I really believe this is what God wants me to do? Am I willing to see it through even if things don't go the way *I* want them to? If not, what's holding me back?

Reality Check: Fact version

◎What skills or gifts do I know I lack but know I need for this thing God has put on my heart to work? Who can use their gifts to help me? Who can I learn from?

◎Whose gifts complement mine? How might I be able to help them accomplish what God has put on *their* hearts?

Go

(about 10 minutes)

If you've chosen **Option A**, *read on.*
If you're doing **Option B**, *go to page 183.*

Here's a test to see if your mission in life is finished—if you're still alive, it's not.

—A.W. Tozer

Close this season together by reading 1 Peter 4:7-11, and then lead everyone in prayer.

prayer⊖

》 **Lord, we thank you for giving us your life—for breaking through the darkness in our lives with your light. There's nothing more important than that. And because of what you've done in our lives, please use our lives to bring glory to you and to reveal your power and goodness to a world that desperately needs to see it.**

Help each of us see how unique we are to you, and help us see what you want to accomplish through each of us. Show us the gifts and passions that truly have come from you and what you want to do with them. Show us the people we need to work with to glorify you. Give us what we lack so we can look back and see the incredible things you've done through us—and maybe even despite us. Open our eyes to see those who need to hear of your love, and those who need to see it in our actions, and prepare us for that work. Give all of us the hearts to allow you to work, and show us how to put our hearts together to accomplish your will. In Jesus' name, amen.

Everybody can be great...because anybody can serve. You don't have to have a college degree to serve. You don't have to make your subject and verb agree to serve. You only need a heart full of grace. A soul generated by love.

—Martin Luther King Jr.

Go Deeper

To dig deeper into how to discover how God is leading—and how to *let* him lead—here are some great resources:

Holy Discontent: Fueling the Fire That Ignites Personal Vision by Bill Hybels (Zondervan)

Called and Accountable: Discovering Your Place in God's Eternal Purpose by Henry T. Blackaby and Norman C. Blackaby (New Hope)

The Call: Finding and Fulfilling the Central Purpose of Your Life by Os Guinness (Word)

The Purpose-Driven Life: What on Earth Am I Here For? by Rick Warren (Zondervan)

The Crucifixion of Ministry: Surrendering Our Ambitions to the Service of Christ by Andrew Purves (InterVarsity)

SEEING IT DIFFERENTLY
Go–Option B

LEADER If you have time, between your reading from 1 Peter (page 181) and the prayer, watch a scene from the movie *The Lord of the Rings: The Two Towers.* Cue the movie to 2:44:22 (DVD Chapter 50), as Frodo slumps down and says, "I can't do this, Sam." Stop the clip at 2:46:33, after Sam says, "That there's some good in this world, Mr. Frodo. And it's worth fighting for."

Let's take a minute now to prepare our hearts for prayer. Where are you thinking, I can't do this? Where have you gotten so wrapped up in "I have to do this" that you can't see the people right alongside you who want to help? Where can't you see far enough ahead to believe God will finish the work started in you? What's the good that's worth fighting for that you need God to renew in your own heart, so you can keep fighting for it?

Allow a minute for everyone to silently prepare their hearts, and then go on to the closing prayer on page 181, which begins, **Lord, we thank you for giving us your life**...

General Tips

- **Read ahead.** Although these sessions are designed to require minimum preparation, read each one ahead of time. Highlight the questions you feel are especially important for your group to spend time on.

- **Preview DVD clips.** The copyright doctrine of fair use permits certain uses of very brief excerpts from copyrighted materials for not-for-profit teaching purposes without permission. If you have specific questions about your intended use of copyrighted materials, consult your church's legal counsel. Your church can obtain a blanket licensing agreement from Christian Video Licensing International for an annual fee. Visit cvli.com, or call 888-771-2854 for information.

- **Enlist others.** Don't be afraid to ask for volunteers. Who knows? They may want to commit to a role such as teaching a session or bringing snacks once they've tried it. However, give people the option to say, "No, thanks" as well.

- **Be prompt.** Always start on time. If you do this from the beginning, you'll avoid the tendency of group members to arrive later and later as the season goes on.

- **Gather supplies.** Make sure to have the supplies for each session on hand. (All supplies are listed on the opening page of each session.) Feel free to ask other people to help furnish supplies. This will give them even more ownership of the session.

- **Discuss child care.** If you're leading a small group, discuss how to handle child care—not only because it can be a sensitive subject but also because discussing options will give your group an opportunity to work together *as* a group.

- **Pray anytime.** Be ready and willing to pray at times other than the closing time. Start each session with prayer—let everyone know they're getting "down to business." Be open to other times when prayer is appropriate, such as when someone answers a question and ends up expressing pain or grief over a situation he or she's currently struggling with. Don't save it for the end—stop and pray right there and then.

- **Let others talk.** Try not to have the first or last word on every question (or even most of them). Give everyone an opportunity to participate. At the same time, don't put anyone on the spot—remind people that they can pass on any questions they're not comfortable answering.

- **Stay on track.** There are suggested time limits for each section. Encourage good discussion, but don't be afraid to "rope 'em back in."

- **Hold people accountable.** Don't let your group off the hook with the assignments in the Walk It Out section— this is when group members apply in a personal way what they've learned. Encourage group members to follow through on their assignments.

- **Encourage group challenges.** Also note that "Do It Together"—the last weekly challenge in Walk It Out—is meant to be done as a group. Make sure that group members who take on these challenges are both encouraged and organized.

- **Pray.** Finally, research has shown that the single most important thing a leader can do for a group is to spend time in prayer for group members. So why not take a minute and pray for your group right now?

Session 1

- Review the General Tips starting on page 185, if you haven't already.

- If this is the first time you're meeting as a group, take a few minutes before your session to agree on a few simple ground rules. Here are three important ones:

  1. Don't say anything that will embarrass anyone or violate someone's trust.

  2. Likewise, anything shared in the group *stays* in the group, unless the person sharing it says otherwise.

  3. No one has to answer a question he or she is uncomfortable answering.

- The opening icebreaker will probably be a little tough at first. It was in our field test. Once we explained, "You can't tell the others in your group what you do," the immediate question was "What *can* we talk about?" Don't tell them. Let them figure it out for themselves. They will. Although perhaps the most interesting answer came from a young newlywed: "I don't know *who* I am right now." And that's what this session (*and* this season) is all about discovering.

- Before you dismiss this first session, make a special point to remind group members of the importance of following through on the weekly challenge each of them have committed to in the Walk It Out section.

Session 2

- If new people join the group this session, use part of the Come and See time to ask them to introduce themselves to the group, and have the group pass around their books to record contact information (page 18). Give a brief summary of the points covered in Session 1.

- If people normally take their shoes off in the home where you meet, ask them to bring their shoes with them. You'll need them for your prayer time at the end of this session.

- For your foot-washing activity: If anyone's wearing stockings, give them permission to leave them on. You're not actually going to *do* a foot washing, but don't let anyone know that—let them sweat it out.

Some people in our field test became very uncomfortable during this activity. Most of it had to do with either washing other people's feet or not wanting their own feet touched, although one person was very worried that she'd have to pray for everyone else in the group. You just don't know what people will become concerned about sometimes. (And she's a very good pray-er, too.)

Of course, you could do a foot washing, if you like. It could well be a profound experience for your group. Here's how to run it:

After your reading from John 13, ask people to take off their shoes and socks. Show the pitcher of water, basin, and towel that you brought today, and say, **Today I'm going to wash your feet.**

If your group is large or time doesn't allow for you to wash everyone's feet, choose only a few people whose feet to wash—having people wonder whether they'll be getting their feet washed or not will still produce the necessary uneasiness. Or use multiple basins and towels (one of each for every 10 to 12 people), and have others help you do the foot washing.

After a person has removed all footwear, place the basin under that person's feet. Gently pour water from the pitcher over his or her feet, catching it in the basin. Then gently blot his or her feet dry with the towel.

Once your foot washing is completed, ask:

- What was it like wondering whether or not I'd actually wash your feet? Why?

- How did you feel when I did? Why?

- When Jesus said his disciples should follow his example, what was he really talking about?

- What makes you uncomfortable or unwilling to serve others? What can help you get past that?

  Afterward say something such as: **Serving others isn't always easy or comfortable, but Jesus showed us not only that we can do it but also to have joy *while* doing it. It can be hard to step out of our comfort zones, but everything Jesus did showed us that it's worth it to follow his example.**

  Go on to Go when you're done.

- The discussion in Go got interesting during our field test. The idea of letting go of your "rights" to serve others struck a chord with many in the group, and they were still talking about it days later. So be sure to explore this idea as a group. Don't just blow through the questions; these are big ones we all need to answer if we truly want to walk out our faith before others.

- On that note, we'd encourage you once more to take advantage of the Walk It Out section. Make it a take-home piece if you have to, so you have enough group time elsewhere. While we suggest doing section in pairs, you can approach it any way you like. In our field test. we did it as an entire group and got a variety of interesting responses—as well as a heightened sense of accountability. (Now *everyone* knows what we committed to!)

Session 3

- Yes, you heard that right—the people who come together as a group at the beginning of Seek and Find will soon discover that they'll be working together for this entire season. And the friendships that emerge (or deepen) from that can last a lifetime. So stick to the plan in the weeks to come.

  By the way, two people in a group is OK, if necessary. And it's preferable to have no more than three. "But what if we get new people or lose people?" We'll talk about that in Session 4.

- Are you praying for your group members regularly? It's the most important thing a leader can do for his or her group. Take some time now to pray for your group, if you haven't already.

Session 4

- Now that you're a month into this season, you may find it helpful to make some notes right after your session to help you evaluate how things are going. Ask yourself, Did everyone participate? and, Is there anyone I need to make a special effort to follow up with before the next session?

- Let's come back to the group dynamic mentioned in Session 3. If you have newcomers this week, try to create new groups from them, if possible. If you only have one new man or woman, add him or her to one of your twosomes. On the other hand, if only one person from a given group has shown up, let him or her join another group this week.

  And while you shouldn't need to worry about it this week, start thinking about this: If all of your groups are already at three and someone new arrives, ask for an existing group to volunteer to get into two sets of two. The idea is not to rearrange groups, but to *birth* them. This is a principle that will serve your group, and your church, well in the future. (Of course, if you're not sure if your visitor is going to stick around, it's OK to let a group be a foursome for a week or two before birthing a new one.)

- About that snack: If you're a Sunday school class, offer something like breakfast burritos, omelettes, or a breakfast casserole. If it's late enough in the day, bring a pizza (or more than one, depending on your group size). Offer at least a couple of different taste choices, such as different toppings or fillings. Send out a reminder during the week for everyone to bring their appetites!

- For extra impact, play some classical music in the background as everyone arrives, and maybe even throughout your meeting time. Aside from creating a relaxing atmosphere, you can also (if you choose) use it as a bridge to discussing how using our spiritual gifts together is like a well-tuned orchestra. Play with the idea however you see fit.

- Some of the spiritual gifts broached in this session are still a topic of discussion among many Christians. We're not getting into those debates. Still it's good to prepare for what might come up.

  For example, there's the issue of gifts of tongues and interpretation. Some view tongues as God's gift to Christians for New Testament times only; others view them as critical gifts that every Christian should possess today; yet others land somewhere between the two poles. Because of their very nature, you *know* whether you possess these gifts or not. You don't need a survey to tell you.

  Likewise, ask 10 Christians for a definition of prophecy, and see what happens. The surveys were constructed to take the various definitions into consideration; still, your church may feel strongly about its particular definition.

  If there's any question about what position your church takes on certain spiritual gifts, talk with your pastor or Christian education leader...preferably before your session.

- During your white board session, write everyone's answers to your first question, thanking them for their responses—even if someone suggests something that's *not* normally considered a spiritual gift. Also try to leave plenty more room to write—you'll need it.

  Our field-test group had a lot of fun with this piece, particularly when we explored the question, "What areas do you see where these gifts complement one another?" People were making both obvious and not-so-obvious connections—which helped set up the next question perfectly as we explored how people who are *not* built like us could help us become more like Jesus.

Session 5

- Remember the importance of starting and ending on time, and remind your group of it, too, if you need to.

- This would be a good opportunity to remind you that if you need to spend more time on a given session than just one week—and if you're not tied to a calendar and *can* spend some extra time—then *do it!* Taking the time to understand what God wants to tell your class, group, or accountability partner(s) is way more important than covering the material.

- For your closing prayer time, consider asking for volunteers to pray for requests that were shared. You could also minimize the time you spend sharing prayer requests by just diving into prayer. Don't tell each other about the requests; just tell God, and let others listen. If certain requests need to be explained later on, spend some time afterward discussing those requests so people know how to pray during the week for one another.

Session 6

- This would be a good time to remind group members of the importance of following through on the weekly challenge each of them have committed to in Walk It Out.

Session 7

- Congratulations! You're halfway through this season. It's time for a checkup: How's the group doing? What's worked well so far? What might you consider changing as you approach the remaining sessions?

- To maximize the impact of this session and the potential it could have both for your group and your church:

  a) Provide a list of ministry opportunities both inside and outside your church to everyone. Talk to your pastor or outreach coordinator beforehand to find out what your church's needs are and who you're currently trying to reach outside your church doors.

b) Likewise, ask those in leadership—whether pastors or ministry leaders—to make time to sit down with individuals in your group and explore areas in which group members have expressed an interest. Even if people aren't sure about their next move yet, try to sit down with each person one-on-one or get them with another leader who could help them explore further.

If you're not ready to do all of the above this week, that's OK. But get the process started. Don't give people all this great information and then leave them hanging—do what you can to help them take the next steps. Help the people in your group discover who they are in Jesus, what God has already given them, and why he's given it to them.

• For those items of personal interest used in Come and See, here are a few ideas: branches (nature); flowers (gardening); a plastic fork (cooking or eating); ticket stubs from a concert, movie, or sports event. Hopefully by now you know enough about your group to come up with more ideas from there. It's OK to have more than one of a given item, if you know that people share certain interests. Make sure they're all things you can part with because you *will*.

Push your group for answers to the question, "If our desires really *are* God's desires, what reasons would God have for *not* fulfilling them?" If necessary, add something such as, "This *isn't* a rhetorical question."

Session 8

• To give extra impact to the domino activity in Seek and Find, wait until groups have set up their sequences and then ask them to remove three to five dominoes from the middle. Then ask them tip over the first domino and see what happens. Wait until the sequence stops falling, and then go ahead and read and discuss 1 John 4:7-21.

Also consider being willing to part with some of your dominoes. Let group members each hang on to the dominoes after your activity. Use them as a prompt in your closing prayer time, then let everyone take them home as reminders of how God's love for them can "topple" into others.

Session 9

- For your snack, a bowl of popcorn or freshly baked cookies would work especially well, as group members would not only see it but also smell it. Also, make sure there's enough left over for everyone to share during your prayer time.

  Display your snack prominently so everyone will notice it as they come in—but make sure no one takes a sample before you begin. Once you're ready, serve yourself—*just* yourself—and begin eating in front of the group. Feel free to play it up a bit. Begin talking as you're eating. Have another bite while you're eating. Take your time. Once you've gotten some (at least facial) reactions, ask, "So what have you been thinking as you've been sitting there, watching me eat?" Once you've gotten responses, begin passing your snack around, and continue your discussion at "When have *you* felt left out?" Save some of your snack so you can share it again during your prayer time.

  So you know: I didn't do it quite the way I described above. I just started eating (a big bowl of popcorn, in our case) and asked, "When have you felt 'left out?' " It was a bit obvious, but our group immediately cracked up over it.

- How are you doing with your prayer time for the group? Take some time to pray for your group now, if you haven't done so already.

Session 10

- For your snack, have enough so everyone can have more than one cookie if they like. Before you meet, bake one-half of your cookie dough. Partially bake some of the remaining cookie dough, and leave some of it totally unbaked.

  Or if you have time, do it the way we did for our field test—one-third unbaked, one-third baked perfectly, and one-third overbaked (but not so burnt as to be inedible). It helped group members understand and illustrate their own spiritual conditions. Some also described themselves as "cooked perfectly in some places, but not others" or "burned on the outside and undercooked inside."

Session 11

- Now is a good time to do another group checkup—especially if you're planning on doing another season together after this one. Ask yourself (and the group, if it makes sense to do so—but phrase it differently if you do), Is everyone participating? and, Is there anyone I need to make a special effort to follow up with?

Session 12

- Since your next session will be the last one of this season, you'll probably want to start discussing with the group what to do after you've completed this season. Will you go on to Season 4? "pull over" for an in-depth study of another subject? break up and head to different classes? Make your plans now.'

- If group members have already worked through Season One of *Growing Out: Growing in Jesus,* encourage them to bring their Personal Mission Statements from Session 13

To order copies of *Season 4: Growing Others,* visit your local Christian bookstore or group.com.

of that season next week. It might help them get a jump on the assignment you'll do together.

- For extra impact: You also could ask group members to buy small gifts for their fellow group members to share next week. This season *is* about gifts, after all. Use this as an opportunity for group members to affirm each other's gifts, joys, abilities, and passions.

Session 13

- Since this is your group's last session in this season, make sure you have a plan for next week and beyond.

- For this closing session, you'll offer foods that feature two or more things that go well together—trail mix, fruit salad, an ice-cream-sundae bar, even peanut-butter-and-jelly sandwiches or omelettes. Or if you're willing to do a little more work beforehand, have the group create its own trail mix. Select your ingredients, and give everyone an assignment; then when everyone arrives, mix up your ingredients, and enjoy them during your discussion time. Whatever you think of—and you know your group will enjoy—go for it!

- You'll also want to plan a way to celebrate your time together. Do something special after class, or plan a separate celebration for another time and place. Your call. No matter what you do—congratulations! You've made it through Season 3 of *Growing Out*! We hope you've been blessed in your walk together these past few months and that you'll continue to let God lead all of you forward together.